George Theodore Baker
Lewis B. Maytag, Jr.
april 1962 to

THE ANATOMY OF AN AIRLINE

Books by Brad Williams

DUE PROCESS

A BORDERLINE CASE

DEATH LIES IN WAITING

MAKE A KILLING

A WELL-DRESSED SKELETON

FLIGHT 967

STRANGER TO HERSELF

THE MYSTERIOUS WEST
  (*with Choral Pepper*)

LOST LEGENDS OF THE WEST
  (*with Choral Pepper*)

THE ANATOMY OF AN AIRLINE

Brad Williams

THE
ANATOMY
OF AN
AIRLINE

1970

Doubleday & Company, Inc.

Garden City, New York

Library of Congress Catalog Card Number 77–100044
Copyright © 1970 by Brad Williams
All Rights Reserved
Printed in the United States of America
First Edition

THE ANATOMY OF AN AIRLINE

PART ONE

CHAPTER ONE

The press conference at the Biltmore Hotel in Los Angeles was well attended by all three divisions of the news media: radio, television, and the press. The date was June 12, 1961, and the target of the newsmen was George Theodore Baker, the blunt-speaking and sometimes abrasive president of National Airlines, which on the previous day had inaugurated service along the Southern Transcontinental Route, extending its system westward from Houston, Texas, to Nevada and California.

Baker sat on a dais, tipped back in his chair, both hands with splayed fingers pressing against his rib cage. He was a short and stocky man in his early sixties, with a square jaw and beard-shadowed jowls, and there was no outward indication that he had been in poor health all his life.

During the early part of the conference Baker was polite but aloof, and he did not deviate from his habit of answering questions in the briefest manner possible, often with no more than a monosyllable. This is a technique that frustrates newsmen, because it makes the subsequent writing of a story difficult. Usually when this happens, the media drift on to a new assignment, no mention is made of the conference, and the publicity persons who arranged it start formulating acceptable answers to the inevitable questions as to why the conference failed.

Sometimes, however, a newsman will needle the subject of

an interview in the hopes of obtaining some newsworthy copy. If the subject responds, the newsmen are delighted, and at this particular conference the needle was finally inserted and Baker responded.

"How many people can you carry in one of your DC-8s?" a reporter asked.

"One hundred and twenty-four."

"How long would it take one plane to make a round trip between Los Angeles and Miami?"

"About eleven hours."

The reporter looked at his notes. "Do you plan to cancel jet service along your East Coast routes?"

"No."

"You said earlier that you estimated the potential number of passengers along this route at about twenty-five thousand a month. National only has three DC-8s, and if you used these night and day along this route, you still wouldn't be able to move twenty-five thousand passengers a month."

Baker again pressed his rib cage with his hands. "We have six more coming from Douglas," he replied. "And may I suggest you look up the meaning of the word 'potential.' "

"It takes a year to build a DC-8," the reporter persisted. "If this potential traffic occurs before you can service it, do you think the Civil Aeronautics Board will put an additional carrier on this route?"

"The route case has been settled by the CAB," Baker retorted, "and we have the equipment to service it."

Another reporter caught Baker's attention. "Some time back, Eastern was awarded this same route," the newsman said. "If I remember correctly, you went to court and got an injunction, which stopped them. Now, what's to prevent Eastern from doing the same thing to you?"

"Your facts are wrong."

"I was here when it happened," the reporter insisted. "It was in this same hotel. They were having a big civic dinner, and just before Rickenbacker got up to speak, he was handed a telegram which stated you had enjoined him from starting service."

Baker smiled. "Now, that may be true." He looked at the reporter for a few seconds, then added, "Eastern was trying to set up an improper interchange. We have already established service and have done it in a proper and legal manner."

"Are you saying that Eastern had been behaving in an illegal manner?"

"No." Baker waved his hand. "National now is serving Los Angeles; Eastern is not."

A television reporter asked, "Do you have any comments on the Channel 10 case?"

"If you steal a chicken, you don't pluck it on the way home."

"Do you anticipate any more problems with the Air Line Pilots union?"

"Of course. Who doesn't?"

"The Civil Aeronautics Board has ordered National to get rid of the four hundred thousand shares of Pan American stock it now holds. How do you propose to do this?"

"Trade it."

There was a pause. One of the television cameramen began to dismantle his equipment, and then another reporter spoke up: "Where's the safest place to be seated in an airplane during a crash?"

Baker did not hesitate. "Flat on your ass," he replied.

For about five seconds there was absolute quiet in the room; the press usually is a cohesive group, and one of the members had been insulted. Then John L. Morris, National's vice president, who had been leaning against the wall, chuckled softly. The chuckle was infectious, and presently everyone in the room was laughing, including the reporter who had asked the question. The interview was over. The cameras were dismantled and the reporters' notebooks folded.

Baker was one of the first to leave the room; yet, when he reached the small foyer of the hotel at the Grand Avenue exit, he waited, watching the newsmen come down the elevator.

When the reporter who had asked him the question about the injunction emerged, Baker strolled over to him. "Were you really at that dinner that Eastern put on?" he asked mildly.

The newsman nodded.

"Where was Rickenbacker?"

"He was at the head table, next to the speaker's lectern."

"Who else was there?"

"It was a very large group. The mayor was at the head table, along with several city councilmen and county supervisors. Rickenbacker got the telegram just before he was going to speak."

"Was he mad?"

"Well, you could see that he was upset."

Baker laughed. "I'll bet he was," he replied as he turned away.

This was a warm day in Los Angeles, and the smog in the downtown section of the city was heavier than usual. Approximately an hour after the press conference had ended, Baker came down from his suite in the Biltmore accompanied by some members of his board of directors and some National officers. The group was being hosted by the Shell Oil Company at a luncheon in the city's exclusive Jonathan Club, where Baker was to speak before several civic and business leaders.

When he came out the Grand Avenue exit, he looked for a taxi, but there were none in the stalls. The Jonathan Club was only a block distant, and someone, obviously unused to the habit patterns of Southern Californians, suggested that they walk.

The Jonathan Club is in the middle of the block on Hill Street, as is the Grand Avenue exit from the Biltmore, and thus the shortest distance between the two points for a pedestrian is to skirt the grounds of the large Los Angeles Public Library and cut through a parking lot. In the middle of the parking lot, Baker suddenly gasped, stretched out both hands to steady himself, then leaned against the fender of an automobile. His companions paused, and, oddly, no one said a word. For about a minute, he rested; then, with a deep sigh, he pushed himself away from the car. "It's this goddam heat," he said mildly. "Or maybe it's the smog."

Baker's speech at the Jonathan Club was very brief. He acknowledged the introduction and thanked his host for the luncheon and the guests for attending. He asked Morris to cancel an appointment he had made to meet with officials of the Douglas Aircraft Corporation that afternoon. When he left the Jonathan Club, he hailed a taxi and rode alone the short distance back to the Biltmore Hotel.

Early in the afternoon of the same day, in Denver, Colorado, G. Ray Woody, the executive vice president of Frontier Airlines, walked into the office of its president, Lewis B. Maytag, Jr., and sprawled into a comfortable chair. Bud Maytag is an exact opposite from the blustery and domineering Baker. Soft-spoken, he has a deceptively shy smile and a quick sense of humor that covers a mind that works with the speed and efficiency of a computer. Baker was round and short, and he smoked thick panatelas. Maytag is tall and lean, and when he does smoke occasionally, his preference is the thin, black Stephano cigarette. Woody, although some years senior to Maytag, is very much like him in thought and attitudes. Like Maytag, Woody is soft-spoken, and he subscribes to the philosophy that a great deal of movement does not necessarily mean a great deal of action.

For the past four years, Maytag had held control of Frontier Airlines. Most of these four years had proved a steady source of frustration to him, because Frontier was a regional carrier, heavily subsidized by the government and thus most rigidly supervised by the Civil Aeronautics Board.

Maytag, grandson of the founder of the Maytag Washing Machine Company, understandably was oriented to the business philosophy that a successful company is one operated profitably for the benefit of its stockholders.

A regional airline within the United States can be compared to Siamese twins joined at the body but with separate, functioning heads. One head is government, the other is corporate management, and the brain within each head attempts to dominate the movement of the body. The motivations of both heads are dictated by logic, but more often than not, they are in conflict.

The posture of the government regulatory agencies is that regional carriers are in existence to provide air-carrier service to communities that need air transportation but do not generate enough traffic to make it profitable for an unsubsidized carrier to service them. This is their function. This is the primary reason for their existence. Rigidly controlled, they lose money through their operations, and the government pays these losses through a subsidy.

Regional carriers, however, are not owned by the government. They are publicly owned. Most managements of regional carriers are motivated by the desire to turn the carrier into a profit-making venture for the benefit of the stockholders. To do this, they must be given long-haul routes, which can be profitable, and turn over air transportation service in the smaller communities to what is known as third-level carriers, which, in effect, are air taxi services. This, too, is a logical premise. If a regional carrier, however, is given a long-haul route, this puts it in competition with trunk carriers, which are unsubsidized. It is government competing against private industry. The two heads of the Siamese twins butt against each other constantly, and Maytag was getting tired of the bruises. Earlier in the year, he had been rebuffed by the CAB in an attempt to sell off the most unprofitable segment of Frontier's route structure to a midwestern regional carrier. Shortly after this, he had decided that the most logical solution to his problem was to sell Frontier and try to buy control of a trunk carrier. This was the subject of the conversation this morning in Denver between Maytag and Woody.

In all but two of the existing trunk carriers within the

United States, the shares of stock were so dispersed that it would be almost impossible for one man to acquire control. The two exceptions were Trans World Airlines and National Airlines. TWA was in such a financial morass that even Howard Hughes, who owned 78% of it, was in trouble. National Airlines, however, which was controlled by George Theodore Baker, and which had just been awarded the potentially rich Southern Transcontinental Route, was a medium-sized trunk carrier. It had a bastard fleet—three DC-8s, with three more to be leased from Douglas in the future, Lockheed Electras, Constellations, DC-6s, DC-7s, Convair 340s, and even one Lockheed Lodestar.

"Still, it can't help but make money," Maytag commented.

Woody agreed. "But it's being mismanaged costwise and policywise. Although its promotion has been particularly good on the East Coast from time to time, it's being run like a toy electric train. I estimate we can cut eight million dollars a year from its costs and thereby improve its profit by that much."

Maytag studied the memorandum that Woody had written on several pages of a yellow, legal-sized notepad. Maytag had considerable respect for his executive vice president. Woody had come to Frontier from TACA, a large Central American carrier, with which he had held a similar position. Earlier, he had been an executive with Waterman Airlines, a TWA pilot, and a stunt pilot in his native West Virginia.

On this day, Maytag knew, National Airlines' stock was selling for about seventeen dollars. Maytag knew also that almost everything is for sale if the price is right, and he wondered if Baker would sell out for thirty to thirty-five dollars a share, double the current price on the New York Stock Exchange. "Have you ever met Baker?" he asked aloud.

Woody shook his head. He had never met Baker but he knew him by reputation. There were stories that he had "taken" the wily Juan Trippe of Pan American on two different occasions, and Baker's feud with Rickenbacker was legendary.

"I don't know him personally," Woody replied, "but I understand he can be very difficult to deal with."

Maytag smiled. "That will make it more interesting," he replied. "How do we approach him?"

Woody had the answer immediately. He knew a man in Chicago named Walter Heller, who was in the factoring business. On one occasion he had loaned TACA some money, and Woody knew that Baker also had been one of Heller's clients. Maytag agreed with Woody that the first overture to Baker should be made through Heller.

"How old is he?" Maytag asked.

"Sixty-one; a little early to retire."

"There's no way the airline can lose money," Maytag said. "No way."

Woody agreed. "Thirty-five dollars a share is a good price for it, however, and Baker just may want to retire young."

During the morning of June 13, Baker moved from the Biltmore to a Beverly Hills hotel. His wife, Irma Wilson, and his only child, Barbara, who had accompanied him to Los Angeles on the inaugural flight, were shopping in Beverly Hills. In the afternoon, Baker went for a walk with a lifelong friend, Lou Bower. On Wilshire Boulevard, Baker once again suddenly staggered, pressed his hands against his chest, then clutched a lamp stanchion for support. His face was pale, but he seemed to recover quickly. He passed the seizure off as a stomach upset. Again he caught a taxicab and was driven back to his hotel.

It was not until several weeks later that Bower realized that his friend, whom he had hired as a teenage boy to repossess cars, probably had suffered two heart attacks in as many days.

CHAPTER TWO

National Airlines is unique in that it is the only major trunk carrier in the United States today that came into being after the airmail scandals of the early thirties. Continental Airlines claims a birth date of 1934, but Continental is an offshoot from the Southwest Division of Varney Airlines, which originally was formed in 1926. The Western Division of Varney Airlines was absorbed by United in 1930.

It has taken less than man's average life span for the airline industry to develop from its puling infancy to the sophisticated maturity of today. There are some who contend that the birth date for commercial aviation was January 1, 1914. On this date, a Tony Janus carried the first paying air passenger on a flight from St. Petersburg to Tampa, Florida, in a Benoist Flying Boat. His passenger was a Mayor Phiel of St. Petersburg, who paid five hundred dollars for the world's first airline ticket and probably established a record never to be broken for revenue passenger miles. A passenger in one of today's jet transports covers the same distance for less than fifty cents.

The Janus operation, however, was little more than an expensive roller coaster, and after a few months, the novelty wore off and the operation folded. It probably would not be remembered today were it not for an annual presentation of a Tony Janus Award by Tampa civic leaders to some prominent aviation figure.

A more proper birth date is May 15, 1918, when the first

plane to carry mail took off from a tiny polo field between the Potomac River and the tidal basin in Washington. Earlier in the year, the Congress had appropriated one hundred thousand dollars for the Post Office Department to experiment with the possibility of carrying mail by air. Three Curtiss JN-4s, better known as Jennies, were requisitioned from the Army and were delivered in crates to the polo field, where they were assembled by the military for the first flight to New York.

President Woodrow Wilson, his wife, and members of the Cabinet were among the many who gathered to witness this historic occasion. Post Office officials asked Wilson to pose by the plane for news photographers. The President did so reluctantly. His hand was still bandaged from burns received in his last publicity appearance, when an Army officer had asked him to pose by a tank. At that time, Wilson had dropped his hand on a hot exhaust manifold.

After the pictures were taken, a Post Office truck bumped its way across the field with the first sack of airmail scheduled for delivery in New York. A few sample letters were passed out to the dignitaries, who presently discovered that the first airmail stamps made in the United States had been printed upside down. (These stamps are so rare today that philatelists have paid more than $4500 apiece for them.) At the time, however, this was considered relatively unimportant, and the mail was loaded.

The pilot adjusted his helmet, climbed into the cockpit, and signaled for a mechanic to spin the propeller to start the engine. The engine did not fire. About three quarters of an hour later, the mechanics diagnosed the cause. No one had fueled the plane. The President fidgeted for about an hour, until this oversight was corrected and the aircraft was able to take off. The eager pilot circled the field, buzzed the reviewing stand, waggled his wings, then lined up on a course headed due south, in the opposite direction from New York, and disappeared over the horizon. Some hours later he ran out of gas and made a successful forced landing. A Post Office truck found him the following day and drove the airmail with the upside down stamps back to Washington.

Subsequent flights were more successful, however, and for the next twenty years, until the creation of the Civil Aeronautics Board, the Post Office Department, through its award of airmail contracts, controlled the development of commercial aviation within the United States. The Post Office Department was the midwife at the birth of National.

Domestically, the four largest airlines in the United States today are United, American, Trans World, and Eastern. United, the biggest in the nation, was put together by Boeing Aircraft through an amalgamation of smaller carriers, primarily as an outlet for its aircraft; American was developed by AVCO; TWA was conceived by Curtiss-Wright, and Eastern was packaged by General Motors. None of the Big Four can be called a pioneer airline. They were stitched and sewn together by big business and financed by the government through the award of airmail contracts.

There are seven other trunk-line domestic carriers within the United States. All but one of these seven surviving carriers came into being during the 1920s and survived incredible pressures from both the government and financial institutions to merge with one of the Big Four. Delta, the fifth largest carrier, is the outgrowth of a crop-dusting company in Georgia. Western almost collapsed on two occasions. Through government pressure, it lost a great part of its route structure to TWA. Later, in order to meet a payroll, it was forced to sell off its Denver–Los Angeles route segment to United. Northwest began with a four-hundred-mile route between Chicago and Minneapolis, and Braniff, Continental, and Northeast had equally modest beginnings.

By 1928, there were forty-four airlines in existence within the United States. In addition, there were innumerable flying services, many of which called themselves airlines, and all were trying to cut into the profits of the Big Four by underbidding them on airmail contracts. There was one exception, the Ludington Line, which operated the original shuttle service between Washington and New York.

It was during the administration of Herbert Hoover that most of these small airlines collapsed. There were other factors that caused this in addition to the stock-market crash of October 1929. The theme of the Hoover era was efficiency, co-operation, and a business philosophy that is diametrically opposed to that which is popular today. Hoover believed that business communities should gather into collective action against "waste and over-reckless competition."

A firm adherent to these policies was Walter Folger Brown, the Postmaster General, and it is he to whom recognition should be accorded as the father of the commercial aviation industry in this country. The title is not given as an accolade, but if Brown had not done what he did, the state of the industry would be much different today.

A disciple of Hoover's premise that only the big and the mighty could bring order out of chaos, Brown turned his attention to the airlines. He was a lawyer from Ohio, and a politician, and at the time Hoover was Secretary of Commerce, Brown had served as his assistant. When Hoover ran for President in 1928, Brown resigned to become his campaign manager, and when Hoover was elected, Brown was named Postmaster General in accordance with the custom. Very shortly after his appointment he discovered that one of his duties was "to encourage commercial aviation and contract for the airmail service."

The contracts to carry the airmail had always been put up for bid. There was no profit in carrying passengers, and all forty-four airlines, with the exception of Ludington, needed the federal postal subsidy in order to survive. Apparently it was Brown's belief that this system of low bidding for public contract to carry the mail did little to encourage commercial aviation, because the larger carriers were unwilling to invest in new equipment when faced with the constant threat of losing an airmail contract.

To Brown, this was a prime example of waste and over-reckless competition. The only way commercial aviation could be advanced in the United States was to eliminate competitive bidding. Airmail contracts should be awarded only to those companies strong enough to contribute to the development of commercial aviation.

United Airlines was big and adequately financed. It was an excellent example of what could be done for the growth of commercial aviation. If there could be three or four large airlines making a healthy profit from government contracts, then the airlines themselves would finance bigger and better equipment, which would contribute to the growth of commercial aviation. Therefore, one of Brown's early acts as Postmaster General was to propose legislation by the Congress that would base mail payments on the capacity that was available, whether it was needed for mail or not. He also sought the elimination of competitive bidding and requested the Congress to allow the Post Office to contract with the carriers by negotiation or to enlarge them by extending their existing routes.

The original Airmail Act of 1925 had been sponsored by a Congressman named Clyde Kelly. Apparently Kelly took umbrage over Brown's failure to consult with him, and he was successful in getting Congress to prohibit the Post Office Department from extending the routes of existing carriers. Brown, however, was successful in getting the legislation through that eliminated competitive bidding for airmail contracts and gave him the authority to contract with the carriers by negotiation.

Brown also found a way to get around Kelly. Although Brown could not extend the routes of the existing carriers, there was no restriction in the new Airmail Act of 1930 that prohibited him from pressuring the lines into merging and setting up transcontinental routes.

At this time, the only transcontinental route in existence

was that of United. It ran from New York to San Francisco, with service to many intermediate points. Brown decided arbitrarily that there should be two more transcontinental routes that would terminate in Los Angeles and New York, with service to intermediate points. The way to do this was to pressure the smaller companies into a merger. Because United had strength through Boeing, Brown turned to AVCO and North American for the sources of capital that would provide competition for United and establish service along central and more southerly transcontinental routes.

For the central route, he chose Transcontinental Air Transport, which was loosely associated with Western Air Express (now Western Airlines) and which would be financed by North American Aviation.

For the more southerly transcontinental route to Los Angeles, he turned to AVCO as the holding company. The combinations of the smaller carriers that were forced to merge for the central route became what is known today as Trans World Airlines. The forced mergers of the smaller carriers for the more southerly transcontinental route, the one owned by AVCO, is the nucleus of American Airlines. The fourth largest carrier, which ran down the Eastern Seaboard of the United States through the heavily populated areas, was Eastern Air Transport, financed by General Motors. Eastern Air Transport now is known as Eastern Airlines. Thus, the Big Four carriers were born.

Some of the smaller carriers that had been pressured into merging into one or another of the Big Four resisted. Among them was Delta, which went back to crop dusting and small charter services, Northwest, and Braniff. Although a large piece of Western Airlines was sliced off and given to Trans World, the Salt Lake–Los Angeles segment remained, and so its entity was preserved. There were others also that survived, such as Colonial, and Chicago & Southern, but their combined route mileage was less than that of Eastern Air Transport. This, basically, remained the status of the airline industry until

1933, when Hoover was turned out by Franklin Delano Roosevelt. Brown was replaced as Postmaster General by James Farley. The Deputy Postmaster General was Harlee Branch.

In 1933, when Roosevelt took office, the junior senator from Alabama was Hugo Black, who today is a justice of the United States Supreme Court. One of the many facets of the New Deal was an investigation by Black of Brown's philosophy of wasteful and reckless competition. Black was as anti-big business as Brown was pro-big business, and one of Black's first acts was to open public hearings into the airmail contracts and activities of the former Postmaster General. He formed his committee before Roosevelt's inauguration, and there have been many charges that the committee was politically inspired to advance the status of Hugo Black. Black was helped immeasurably by the late Fulton Lewis, Jr., who at the time was a young reporter working for Hearst.

The Ludington Line, which ran the shuttle between New York and Washington every hour on the hour, was one of the carriers that had been pressured by Brown into merger. Ludington had attempted to secure the airmail contract between New York and Washington, but it had been awarded to Eastern Air Transport despite the fact that Eastern's bid was three times higher than Ludington's. According to Charles J. Kelly, Jr., a former CAB attorney, and author of "The Sky's the Limit," Fulton Lewis, Jr., unearthed this story but was blocked by Hearst from running it. Lewis then slipped his evidence to Black, giving Black the opportunity and the evidence on which to base his crusade against the practices of big business. Brown had awarded the mail contract to Eastern on condition that Eastern buy out Ludington, the same method he had used to force merger of all the other smaller carriers.

As with most Congressional investigations, the "scandal" was blown way out of proportion to the act, but it was a fact that the three largest aviation holding companies, Boeing,

AVCO, and North American, held twenty-four of the twenty-seven federal airmail contracts. Black proved also that lower bids by smaller operators over certain routes had been rejected and that the awards had gone to much higher bids from the major carriers. In every instance, Brown had made it a condition of the transaction that the smaller carrier be purchased by the larger carrier.

The result of the Black investigation was a quick and abrupt termination of all airmail contracts by President Roosevelt. According to Kelly, Roosevelt asked Brigadier General Benjamin Foulois if the Army Air Corps were capable of carrying the mail. Foulois, a political general, told Roosevelt there would be no problem, and thus, within the first few weeks of his assumption of office, Roosevelt took all the airmail contracts away from the carriers and turned them over to the Air Corps. It was a foolish answer that had been given by Foulois, and because of it Roosevelt made a foolish decision. Within one week, the Air Corps had killed twelve pilots, and six more were seriously injured attempting to fly the mail. The average cost of flying the mail by the airlines had been fifty-four cents per mile. The cost of flying the mail by the Army was $2.21 per mile.

It was not long before Roosevelt sought new legislation that would take the airmail back from the Army Air Corps and return it to private hands. Senator Hugo Black, who had triggered the investigations, spearheaded the resulting Air Mail Act of 1934 through Congress. It reopened all airline routes to competitive bidding and forced the manufacturers to divest themselves of their carriers. United split from Boeing, American left AVCO, and North American sold TWA to the Atlas Corporation and the Lehman Brothers. All the airmail routes were put up for competitive bidding. The Big Four of the airline carriers successfully bid on many of the routes. Those carriers that had survived and resisted merger, such as Delta, Braniff, and Northwest, successfully bid for the routes over the smaller areas they served.

At this time, George Theodore (Ted) Baker was living in Chicago, and like most of the rest of the population in the country, he considered himself "broke." Ten years earlier, he had bragged that he would be a millionaire by the time he was forty. Now he had six years to go and he was so far from reaching his goal that, a few weeks before the passage of the Air Mail Act of 1934, he had written to his former business partner, Lou Bower, who had moved to Miami, Florida, to ask if Bower could get him some kind of job with Pan American Airways.

Baker had not been reduced to selling apples, however. He owned two Ryan monoplanes, similar to the one in which Lindbergh had flown the Atlantic, a Butler monoplane, and a Model A Ford.

Shortly after the passage of the Act, however, Baker had an idea. He would bid on some small airmail routes and service them with his Ryans. There was a problem. The Post Office Department was returning the airmail contracts to the established airlines, and it did not appear likely that the officials of the department would award an airmail contract to an airline that would not come into existence until after the contract was let, no matter how small the route. Nevertheless, he had the equipment, which bore on the fuselage the name National Airlines Taxi System. Possibly, this would qualify his bid.

On May 18, 1934, Baker wrote another letter to Bower.

"The National Airlines Air Taxi System is going to bid on two mail contracts to be opened in Washington on May 25. The runs bid on are from Cleveland, Ohio, to Nashville, Tennessee, and from St. Petersburg, Florida, to Daytona Beach, Florida. If you have any influence that can be used in the Post Office Department in Washington with James A. Farley or Harlee Branch, it might be helpful. The mail contract would put me on my feet and help me get straightened around. If we could get the run from St. Petersburg to Daytona Beach,

I would live in Florida, and between us we could make some money."

Farley, a former mayor of Chicago, was the newly appointed Postmaster General. Harlee Branch, a former reporter from Atlanta, Georgia, was Deputy Postmaster General in charge of airmail.

Bower made a telephone call. By coincidence, both Farley and Branch were scheduled to arrive in Chicago for a series of political meetings. Bower caught a train for Chicago, arriving there on Wednesday, the 23rd, two days before the bids were to be opened.

CHAPTER THREE

No one can remember precisely when the meeting occurred, but it was on a warm day in the early part of June 1934 on board a yacht named the *Zenith,* which was moored in one of Chicago's more exclusive yacht basins. The guest of honor was James A. Farley, and among the many persons present were Branch, Bower, a Chicago politician named Charles Weber, and Baker.

The idea of being broke is a relative thing. In the late spring of 1934, to the man on the bread line the thought that any person who owned three airplanes, a Model A Ford, and a half interest in a loan company and who was invited for cocktails aboard a large yacht would consider himself broke was incomprehensible. To Baker, however, there was no doubt as to his insolvency. One of his airplanes, the Butler, had been repossessed by the finance company he owned with Bower. He was delinquent on his hangar fees at Midway Airport. The two Ryans presently were tied down on a small airstrip at Lake Geneva, Wisconsin. Both were for sale, and had been for more than a year.

The National Airlines Air Taxi System came into being shortly after the stock-market crash of 1929. The company was entirely owned by Baker, and until the repeal of the Volstead Act it had operated profitably. Most of its business came from customers who wanted to fly into nearby Canada, where the whiskey was legal, unadulterated, and inexpensive.

Many stories have been circulated that Baker often returned from these trips with a heavy load of cargo. Those who knew Baker at that time say this is not true but that privately he enjoyed the legend. The only time he ever denied the rum-running accusation was before a Civil Aeronautics Board hearing many years later, and the denial was made in an oblique manner. He was asked if he had ever flown rum into Florida from Puerto Rico during the Prohibition era.

"My first trip to Florida was in 1934," Baker replied, "and this was long after the repeal of Prohibition."

Baker was a stocky man with a pugnacious jaw, which gave him an appearance of toughness. It was difficult to tell from his appearance that he was not in good health. He had been a sickly child, suffering from chronic bronchitis and two attacks of pneumonia before he was fifteen. He was also a diabetic. Aside from his health, however, he had been brought up in comfortable circumstances. His father, an English immigrant, was circulation manager for the Chicago *Daily News,* and the Baker family lived in a large house in Ravenswood, on the north side of Chicago. They were the first family to own an automobile in Ravenswood, and they also had a lake-front summer home in Pullman, Michigan.

The car fascinated Ted Baker. On several occasions he tried unsuccessfully to get it out of the garage. Finally he managed to get possession of the keys long enough to have a duplicate set made by a locksmith, but on his first excursion he had the bad luck to pass his father in the downtown section of the city. For months afterward, his father would check the radiator of the car immediately upon his return home to see if it was warm.

There was another incident that occurred in his childhood that apparently made a much greater impression upon Ted Baker than the tanning he received for borrowing his father's car. This occurred during one of the summer vacation periods at Pullman. He and a friend caught a chicken at a farm on the lake shore opposite the Baker cottage. While his friend rowed,

Baker sat in the stern of the boat, plucking and dressing the captured fowl. About an hour later, a farmer arrived at the Baker cottage with a mild suggestion that Ted pay for the fowl.

"What makes you think I took it?" Baker asked.

The farmer pointed to the lake. There was not a breath of wind, and the water was as smooth as a satin sheet. Lying on the water surface and in a straight line from one shore to the other was a string of chicken feathers. Baker paid for the bird, and then for a long time he stared at the feathers until a slight breeze came up and pushed them away.

The official corporate history of National Airlines states that, after Baker was graduated from high school in Chicago, he attended the Montana School of Mines, then worked for the United States Forest Service. There is, however, no record of him ever being enrolled in the Montana School of Mines, and an exhaustive search of the files of the United States Forest Service turns up no indication that he ever was on its payroll. If he did go to Montana, his stay there was of short duration, because he was eighteen when he enlisted in the United States Army, where he served a year domestically, reportedly in a tank battalion. At the end of World War I he was discharged; he returned to Chicago, and on a spring morning walked into the offices of Louis E. Bower, Auto Finance, an automobile loan company, and asked for a job repossessing cars.

"I hired him," Bower said, "because he looked tough, spoke like a gentleman; and that is the perfect combination for a bill collector. Later I found out that he was really tough. He could give you a tongue lashing and come up like a hurricane."

Baker did not remain a car repossessor very long. Within two years Bower sold him part of the business, and three years after this the name of the firm was changed to Bower and Baker when the latter became a full partner. When Baker bought into the business, Bower took a note for part of the payment, but he has no idea where Baker got the rest of the money. He thinks it came from a loan by the senior Baker.

Shortly after the partnership was established, Baker married Bower's attractive, dark-haired secretary, Ruth Yore, and it was about this time that he first became interested in flying.

Baker reported on several occasions that he "caught the bug" after being given a ride at Midway Airport by a barnstormer named Nemo Black. This may be true, but Bower and E. J. Kershaw, who was to become a lifetime pilot for Baker, remembers this somewhat differently.

"Before he bought in," Bower said, "we just financed automobiles. Then he wanted to finance boats, and that paid off, and then one day a man came in and he wanted to finance an airplane. Ted went over to Midway with this guy, and when he came back he had taken his first ride in an airplane. From then on, we started financing airplanes. It was a good business. When the (stock market) crash came in 1929, we only had to take back one airplane, but we had to take back a sack of automobiles."

Kershaw met Baker when he was an instructor at a flying school in Midway. "I thought I gave him his first flight," Kershaw said. "But maybe it was just his first lesson."

Either way, Baker became enamored with airplanes, but although he enjoyed flying them, he always thought of them as mechanical devices that should be utilized to make money. He loved cars, and when he had money, he bought expensive vehicles. He loved boats, and he owned expensive boats, but he never bought an airplane as a personal possession.

After he learned to fly, he acquired an Eastman Flying Boat franchise, which he kept only so long as the flying boats were delivered to him on consignment. On at least three or four occasions he used these flying boats for charter work, a habit which upset the manufacturer to the point where he asked Baker to contribute more than a mooring buoy on Lake Geneva. Baker gave up the franchise.

The party on board the *Zenith* that night was of a social nature. Baker met both Branch and Farley, and Bower recalls that Baker mentioned to Branch that he had bid for two airmail routes and asked when the decision on the awards would be announced. Branch did not know, but indicated it would not be long.

"He told Ted that if his bid was low and that if he had the ability and equipment to perform the service," Bower said, "that he would get the award regardless of whether he owned an airline or not."

Baker lost in his bid for the Cleveland–Nashville airmail route, but he was successful in his bid to connect St. Petersburg and Daytona Beach, Florida. The news came to him by telephone one evening when he was visiting his parents in Ravenswood.

"Now that I've got it, I don't know what to do with it," he told his sister, Mrs. Robert Weiland, when he had hung up.

There had been only one other bid for the one-hundred-forty-six-mile route across Central Florida. This had been made by Gulf Airlines, which, although it was incorporated, owned no equipment and was counting on the postal subsidy to put it in business. Gulf's bid on the route was twenty cents per mile. Baker's winning bid was seventeen cents per mile.

Incredibly, Eastern Airlines, which served Florida, failed to bid for the route. It was an oversight that was to cause the voluble Eddie Rickenbacker, then general manager of Eastern, a large amount of grief in the ensuing years. There has never been a satisfactory answer as to why Eastern did not bid on the route. The carrier was well established; it was expanding aggressively by bidding on other routes for a much lower figure than that submitted by Baker. Within a matter of weeks after the National Airlines System was flying its tiny planes across the State of Florida, Eastern was devoting a considerable effort toward putting it out of business.

Two weeks after Baker was officially granted his certificate, the Bower-Baker Finance Company was liquidated. One of the Ryans was sent south with Kershaw at the controls, the other with a Don Franklin as pilot. Baker flew down in the

Butler, and his wife followed at a much slower pace in the Model A Ford.

The airline became operative on October 15, 1934. Within two months Baker approached Gulf Airlines with a proposal to merge.

CHAPTER FOUR

The telephone call from Walter Heller in Chicago to Ray Woody in Denver came during the latter part of June. It had taken a little longer to reach Baker than Heller had anticipated, because Baker apparently had not returned directly to Miami after the inaugural flight to Los Angeles.

Heller had been frank with the mercurial president of the airline, which was as Woody had wanted it. He had told Baker that Maytag was interested in acquiring control of National and wanted an opportunity to meet Baker to discuss the matter with him and possibly make him an offer. Baker hesitated for a second, then replied, "Fine. Have Mr. Maytag call me."

The Post Office Department, still hypersensitive to public reaction over its experience with the Army Air Corps, demanded that proving runs be made over any new mail route granted. Pilots were required to land at all the fields along the route, including those that might be utilized for emergency landings. After three such flights had been made and the pilots had drawn crude maps of each airport to prove their familiarity with the route, the airline was certificated to carry passengers over its new system.

All operations were conducted during the day. Instruments did not exist. The two Ryans with which the airline was started were slightly modified versions of the "Spirit of

St. Louis," but they were remarkably unsophisticated machines in comparison with the DC-2s and Boeing 247s operated at this time by other carriers within the United States. They ran at either full throttle or not at all. One Ryan could carry four passengers, the other five. This unprepossessing fleet arrived in St. Petersburg in the middle of July, each plane carrying a couple of footlockers full of spare parts. A few days later, a third pilot, Horton Hale, arrived from Chicago by train.

Hale, Kershaw, and Franklin began overhauling the two airplanes, for in those days a pilot was expected to be a mechanic as well as a ticket seller. One of the first things that was done was to repaint the name on the fuselage, dropping the words "Air Taxi," thus making the name of the carrier "National Airlines System." The airline's first employee was hired during this period. He was a youngster "that just hung around the planes," and without anyone actually becoming aware of it he soon was working full time. This was not a difficult accomplishment, as the youngster, David Amos, was paid nothing. Today, he is director of personnel for National Airlines and the only employee of the organization for whom the personnel department does not have an accurate starting date.

Baker, meanwhile, spent most of his time during this period "making contacts" and spreading the word that St. Petersburg had its own airline. He learned very shortly after his arrival that another airline had been formed in the St. Petersburg-Tampa area, that it had been incorporated, that most of its stockholders were prominent citizens in the area, and that these citizens were rather disappointed that Baker had underbid them for the airmail route.

The airline was Gulf Airlines, and its president was Jerome A. Waterman, an executive with the Maas Brothers Department Stores, a large chain in the Tampa area. The original intent of Gulf Airlines was to form an extension to Pan American Airways at Miami through an interchange agreement that would link Miami to Tampa and across the Gulf to New Orleans. When Gulf failed to reach an agreement with Pan

American, it tried to become an operating carrier by bidding on the St. Petersburg–Daytona Beach route, but it was underbid by Baker by eight cents.

On October 15, 1934, the National Airlines System officially inaugurated service across the state of Florida. There was very little, if any, money in the cash register. The income of the three pilots had dwindled to the same level as that of Dave Amos. Ruth Baker was washing antimacassars from the backs of the aircraft seats in the same wash as her husband's shirts. (The marriage only had about a year more to run. The Bakers were divorced in 1935. She presently lives in Key West, Florida.)

The airline operated the first five days of its existence without a passenger. On the sixth day, a Saturday, an attractive young woman appeared at the hangar. She was expensively dressed and quite nervous about her plans to fly to Daytona Beach, but, she explained, it was imperative that she get there as soon as possible. Baker wrote out her ticket, then gaped at the hundred-dollar bill she tendered for payment. There was less than twenty-five dollars in the till. The woman had nothing smaller.

Baker sent Amos to various merchants nearby, but this was during the middle of the Depression, and some of the persons Amos asked to change it had never seen a hundred-dollar bill. Baker delayed the flight and sent Amos into downtown St. Petersburg in the Model A Ford. An hour later, Amos returned. The banks were closed. No merchant could change it. The pretty, young passenger was becoming impatient as well as nervous.

Baker drew Amos aside. "Ride with her over to Daytona Beach and see if you can get it cashed over there," he said.

Amos did as he was told, but a hundred-dollar bill was as rare during the Depression on the east coast of Florida as it was on the west coast. Amos reported his lack of progress by telephone to Baker.

"Then stay with her until the banks open on Monday, but get that fare," Baker replied.

How closely Amos followed the orders is probably known only to him and the attractive young lady involved. Amos returned to St. Petersburg the following Monday with the fare, collected in full.

The mysterious young woman with the hundred-dollar bill "broke the ice," and the load factor slowly increased. Within six months after National Airlines System inaugurated service, it had carried a total of 193 passengers. Early in 1935 there came a day when there were more passengers than there were seats. Within the ensuing week, the same situation happened three times and at both terminal points on the system. With this increase in traffic came the disquieting rumor that Gulf Airlines was planning to go into business and start service in competition with National between St. Petersburg and Daytona Beach. As the rumors persisted, Baker became more nervous. He had two planes capable of carrying a total of nine passengers, planes that were old, and if he was given any competition, he could easily be put out of business.

There was basis for the rumors. At this time, Gulf Airlines' board of directors had been considering three alternatives as to the future of their paper carrier. One was to bankrupt the corporation. Another was to try to reopen negotiations with Pan American. The third, and most appealing, was to raise additional capital and start service throughout Florida on various routes, including the one operated by National. There were no regulations prohibiting this, although the chances of survival were risky without a postal subsidy. On the other hand, the Gulf directors thought, if National could be put out of business, Gulf could probably bid successfully for the airmail subsidy presently held by National. The Gulf Airlines board knew from appearances that Baker was poorly financed, but it did not know if he had the capability to raise enough money to stay in business and make the experiment a risky one for Gulf. While the board debated, Baker went to Chicago.

"He got financial assistance from a man named Harry Parker, a friend of his father's who owned the Flash-Tric Sign Company in Chicago," Bower says.

How much money Baker borrowed from Parker is unknown, but there was a sufficient amount to finance the purchase of two secondhand trimotored Stinson transports from Western Airlines. The two planes were quickly ferried to Florida and painted with the National Airlines System colors.

Baker then wrote to Waterman: "One of our new Stinson trimotor ships will be at the Tampa Airport on Saturday, April 20, at 2:00 p.m., and we would like to have you take a flight over Tampa, Davis Island, and surrounding country as our guest, so that you may know at first hand the type of equipment used on our line. I trust I may have the pleasure of meeting you personally."

Baker did meet Waterman personally, and one of the first questions he asked concerned Waterman's future plans for Gulf Airlines.

"We have reached no decision," Waterman replied evasively.

"What do you currently have in the way of assets?"

Waterman smiled. "At the moment our tangible assets consist of little more than twelve hundred dollars in cash, a couple of typewriters and desks, and an adding machine. Are you suggesting a merger?"

"Exactly."

"Why?"

"The good will that Gulf Airways enjoys here would be a decided asset to National," Baker replied in a disarming tone. He went on to explain that National had the greater assets, in that it had a subsidized route and equipment flying it and thus the stockholders from Gulf would benefit more from a merger. He talked about it for almost a half hour at the conclusion of the flight, then left after telling Waterman that he would outline a proposal that Waterman could take to his directors for consideration.

Baker had demonstrated dramatically that he had finances and that he had uncannily anticipated what was going on in the minds of the board of directors at Gulf. In later years, Baker delighted in telling the story that the idea of merger occurred to him only after he had learned from Waterman that Gulf had twelve hundred dollars in the bank, but Waterman didn't believe it. The Gulf board of directors, after hearing Waterman's report, seriously began to think of merger with National as an alternative to making their own carrier operative.

The airmail leaving St. Petersburg and Tampa had to be carried across the state to Daytona Beach, because this was the only air route serving the two cities. In Daytona Beach, the mail was re-sorted and taken by Eastern Airlines to its destinations in the north, or south to Miami. In the spring of 1935, this distribution came to an abrupt halt. A local utility company, installing new service to the airport, strung some unlighted wires across one end of the runway. An Eastern DC-2, taking off in the dark, ran into them and crashed.

At this time, the Daytona Beach airport was a marginal operation for aircraft as large as the DC-2, and because of the accident and a short runway, Eastern asked the Post Office Department to suspend service until conditions could be improved. The request was readily granted, as was anticipated. What was not anticipated was Baker's reaction to the temporary suspension. The curtailment of Eastern service at Daytona meant that airmail originating in Tampa-St. Petersburg had to be carried by train either to Jacksonville or Miami before it could be placed on an airplane. This could result in a disastrous dip in National's revenues.

Baker responded by immediately seeking authority on a temporary basis to carry the mail from Daytona Beach to Jacksonville, pointing out the hardships Eastern's suspension was causing in the Tampa area. The Post Office thought the argument a valid one and, over Eastern's objections, temporarily extended National northward to Jacksonville.

During this period, the negotiations for the merger between the National Airlines System and Gulf Airlines continued, but in a most erratic manner. Waterman found it most difficult to get any kind of concrete proposal from Baker, and along with other members of the Gulf board of directors, had reached the conclusion that Baker was using the merger discussions only as a ploy to prevent Gulf from entering into competition with him.

The Butler monoplane that Baker had brought from Chicago was worthless for airline operation and had remained, tied down and unused, at the St. Petersburg airport. In January of 1935 Baker impulsively traded it for a secondhand cabin cruiser. The Butler was about eight years old, and its market value was far below the twelve hundred dollars owing on it when it was repossesed. Baker thought he had made a sharp trade until, on the first experimental voyage around Tampa bay, he discovered that the cruiser had a cracked engine block. Aside from this, the cruiser was a comfortable vessel when moored at a St. Petersburg dock, and it was on board this craft that Waterman met with Baker to suggest that either he come up with a written proposal on the merger he had suggested some eight months earlier or face the very strong probability that Gulf would enter into competition against him. Baker promised to have his proposition in the hands of Waterman's attorney, Louis W. Petteway, within six weeks. Although Waterman thought six weeks was somewhat longer than necessary, another delaying tactic by Baker, he had grown to like the blunt-spoken young man from Chicago, and he agreed to Baker's suggestion.

Apparently there is no record of Baker's proposal, but it is known that it infuriated Petteway. On August 21, 1935, the lawyer wrote to Waterman, who was staying at the Biltmore Hotel in New York City.

"I have not submitted this proposition to any of the stockholders, because I do not feel, in the first place, that you would approve of it. In the second place, Sid [Sidney C. Brown, Petteway's law partner] does not approve of it, and in the third place I do not approve of it. In the fourth place, I think we ought to jump on this fellow with both feet. We might get more pleasure out of fighting him than we would profit from this merger.

"I think the fellow is bluffing and I think his bluff can be called; however, I realize your position with reference to protecting the stockholders. Your desire to protect them is no stronger than mine; however, inasmuch as you personally raised most of the money, you perhaps feel a more personal obligation to protect them if you can. If you want to complete this merger, Sid and I will go ahead and play ball with you as we have in the past. If you think well of it, you might take this proposal to Pan American and see what they think about it."

Despite Petteway's reaction, the merger between Gulf Airlines and National Airlines System eventually was accomplished, although it took almost two years, and Baker's motivations for going along with it undoubtedly were much different from his original reasons. According to Bower, Baker had decided that it was necessary to incorporate, and it was cheaper and more advantageous to do it by merging with a paper airline. National was growing larger. Its gross revenues had increased although its profits were still slim. It had reached a point in strength, however, where Baker felt he could successfully combat any competition from Gulf if it became an operational carrier.

Baker signed the merger agreement on August 14, 1936. The terms of the agreement called for the National Airlines System "to set over, transfer, and assign to Gulf Airlines Incorporated all National assets including the planes and equipment now in use, all contracts of whatsoever kind and description, good will, and other such assets, but not including any monies such as the National Airlines System may be possessed of at this time."

The agreement called for the charter of Gulf Airlines to be amended, changing its capital stock setup so as to provide for the issuance of ninety thousand shares of common stock, Class A, with a par value of ten dollars per share and with the privilege of electing three directors. Ten thousand shares of Class B stock were to be issued to Baker. This carried a preference of 5% to dividends before any payment of dividends to Class A stockholders, and the holder of the Class B stock was entitled to name four members to the seven-member board. The stockholders of Gulf were to pay all costs incurred by the revamping of the corporation. The current holders of preferred and common stock of Gulf Airlines would receive two shares of the new Class A stock for each one held of the old. Baker would be president and treasurer of the new corporation.

Although the agreement to merge was signed, a group of Gulf Airlines' stockholders now objected to the proposal. This group felt that it was still possible to raise the necessary capital to become operational and run National out of business. One stockholder objected on sentimental grounds. If the two companies were to merge, the surviving carrier should be known as Gulf Airlines. Nor did Baker appear to be in any hurry to consummate the agreement.

In May of 1937 Baker was successful in another airmail bid, this time for a route from St. Petersburg to Miami, with service to Sarasota and Fort Myers. Inauguration of the new service was scheduled to start in July. A month before the service was scheduled to begin, Baker took delivery of his first new aircraft, a ten-passenger Lockheed Electra. With this, the opposition to the merger from the Gulf stockholders collapsed. The opportunity to "jump on this fellow with both feet" had passed. When Waterman called Baker to suggest that the merger be consummated, he found Baker eager "to get this matter settled."

Baker had good reason to co-operate now. About the time his new Electra was delivered, Rickenbacker announced that Eastern was applying to the Post Office Department for permission to connect Atlanta and Miami via Tampa. This could prove disastrous, as Eastern could easily outschedule National between Tampa and Miami and at the same time seriously erode the airmail subsidy on northbound segments of the route.

Baker met with the Gulf board of directors in mid-June of 1937. There was only one minor note of discord. One of the directors insisted that the name of Gulf Airlines be retained.

Baker disagreed. "Some day this carrier will have routes all over the country," he said. "The National name will be much more appropriate."

The director was stubborn, and a compromise eventually was reached. The name of the carrier was to be known as Gulf National Airlines, and as such it would be incorporated. The incorporation date for the merged carriers was July 8, 1937. The writer has been unable to determine when the "Gulf" was dropped officially, if ever, but so far as Baker was concerned, it never existed. He completely ignored the feelings of the sentimentalist. Stationery that was printed immediately after the merger identifies the airline in the manner by which it has been known since—National Airlines Incorporated.

Baker benefited immensely from the merger in that, although he incorporated for virtually nothing, he had ten thousand shares of stock with a paper value, at least, of a hundred thousand dollars. He now had the additional support of many prominent citizens in the Tampa-St. Petersburg area who had a direct financial interest in the airline and could help him immeasurably in his pending battle with Rickenbacker.

He had incurred some small legal bills in connection with

the transaction. His attorney was Harry Duncan, of the firm of Duncan and Hamlin, in Tavares, Florida, and Duncan had been recommended to Baker by his old friend Lou Bower.

Shortly after the merger with Gulf Airlines was effected, Duncan and Bower were visiting Baker on his boat in St. Petersburg. Duncan complimented Baker on the appearance of the vessel.

"I owe you some legal fees, Harry," Baker replied. "If you can make up your mind right now, I'll make a deal with you. You cross off what I owe you and I'll sign over the boat to you."

"Does it run?"

"The engine needs a little work." Baker held up his hand. "You've got to decide right now."

"It's a deal," Duncan said.

Two days later, after allowing time for Baker to remove his personal possessions from the cruiser, the lawyer came to the dock to look over his boat. There was little to see. Only the flying bridge was above water. Today, no one remembers what made it sink, but Waterman recalls Baker's comment when he was told about it.

"I got rid of it just in time," Baker said.

CHAPTER FIVE

It had been raining in Miami, and the heat and the humidity were both very high, contrasting sharply with the mile-high dry air in Denver, and the thought occurred to him that it was like stepping fully dressed into a sauna bath. The arm over which his garment bag was slung became wet from perspiration before he reached the bottom of the steps. Here a well-dressed woman met him and asked in a French accent if he were Mr. Maytag, and when he nodded, she motioned for him to step into a covered Cushman golf cart.

"Are you with the Maytag Washing Machine Company?" she asked as she drove him beside the long finger ramp toward the terminal building.

"No," he replied truthfully, not volunteering that he was a grandson of the founder. Only a small portion of his life had been spent in Newton, Iowa, where the appliances were manufactured. He had been born in Rochester, Minnesota, and had lived for most of his life in Colorado. The thing he remembered most vividly about Newton were the long hours spent at a piano, playing the scales in an attempt to live up to his mother's hopes that he become a concert pianist.

The golf cart pulled into the lower level of the terminal. The woman asked for his baggage checks, and he indicated that he was carrying all his luggage, thanked her, and went out to the cab stand.

The general offices of the airline were housed in a modern,

three-story building a short distance from the terminal, on the opposite side of a divided highway with a barrier in its center. In order to reach the building entrance the taxi driver left the road, drove in between two motels and across an open field that returned him to the highway headed in the opposite direction, and presently pulled up in front of a parked Jaguar in front of the building. There seemed to be something odd about the building, and Maytag studied it for a moment before he realized that almost all the windows were shaded oddly. They seemed to be the old-fashioned kind of shades that are pulled down on rollers.

Baker's office was on the second floor, and Baker met him at the door, then sat down behind his desk, tipped back in his chair, and pressed his open hands against his chest. For a while they talked of trivial problems in the industry, until Maytag realized it was up to him to make the opening gambit.

"I came down to see if you have any interest in selling your control of National."

Baker tipped farther back in his chair. "Well," he replied, "I don't have any interest in wanting to sell." He paused, then added, "Of course, anything is for sale."

Maytag nodded and waited.

"It would have to be a hell of a premium before I would even consider it," he said after a while.

"What kind of a premium are you talking about? The stock's about seventeen dollars today."

"Oh, it would have to be at least thirty-five or forty dollars a share before I would even consider it."

"Well, that doesn't mean I would be out of the picture."

"You already have an airline. You can't own two."

"I know."

Baker swung around in his chair and looked out the window. He remained in this position for almost a full minute before he turned around again to face Maytag. "Who are you fronting for?" he asked bluntly.

"I don't front for anyone."

For another long moment Baker stared at his guest, then he shrugged slightly. "You know damn' well the CAB isn't going to let you own two airlines."

"I know," Maytag repeated.

"Then you come in here without any CAB problems and I'll talk to you about it. You follow this route and I'll go."

"That's what I came down to find out," Maytag replied quietly.

The conversation once again turned toward trivia, and a little less than an hour after he had entered the office, Maytag departed. The long trip had been well worth the effort, because he had learned that National Airlines was indeed for sale. The next step was to tie up Baker with some kind of option that would block the sale of National to someone else before Frontier was sold.

Maytag walked across the second-floor foyer and glanced into a huge room filled with occupied desks. Apparently the majority of people at National worked in the open. He started to turn toward the elevator, then paused and looked back into the room. The "shades" he had seen from the street were not shades at all. They were long strips of brown wrapping paper gummed over the windows with masking tape.

It was shortly after National Airlines became a corporation that Eastern Airlines began showing visible signs of annoyance toward Baker and the carrier that theretofore had been thought of as little more than a scheduled air taxi. Apparently the friction started when the Post Office Department called for bids on a new airmail route between Jacksonville, Florida, and New Orleans, Louisiana. National and Eastern were among the bidders for the route.

By this time, the runways at Daytona Beach had been extended to a sufficient length to handle operations by DC-2 and DC-3 equipment. Understandably, Eastern asked for restoration of its certificate to provide service between Jacksonville and Daytona Beach, the route that had been temporarily given to National after the Eastern accident. The request was granted. It is reasonable to assume that Rickenbacker thought Baker would withdraw his bid for his New Orleans route because, if he were successful, it would result in his operating two separate and unconnected airlines. With no connecting route between Daytona Beach and Jacksonville, National would be forced to ferry its planes between Jacksonville and its maintenance base in St. Petersburg. If he did continue pressing for the route, he would be forced to bid high in order to compensate for his increased costs.

Shortly after the Gulf merger was effected, Baker wrote to Rickenbacker implying that National would be receptive to merger discussions. As the Gulf merger had been effected to gain powerful support in Tampa to fight the Eastern proposal to enter the Tampa–Miami market, Baker's motivations in writing the letter are obscure. Waterman thinks the letter was no more than an attempt to "needle" Rickenbacker, and in view of the subsequent events, Waterman probably is right.

Rickenbacker responded to the letter by sending his general traffic manager, Paul H. Brattain, to St. Petersburg to discuss the matter.

Baker kept the emissary waiting for three quarters of an hour before he stepped out of his office to meet him. "You go back and tell Rickenbacker not to send an office boy on a man's errand," he said, and turning, he went back into his office and shut the door.

The fuming Brattain followed Baker's suggestion and so lit the fuse to a lifelong feud between the two men. Baker reported later that he received an even more terse reply the next day by telephone from an angry Rickenbacker. "You get the hell out of my way or I'll run you over."

Baker was delighted. There probably was nothing he enjoyed more than a fight, and when the opportunity for one was presented, he played it with the enthusiasm of a fly fisherman who has hooked a large trout.

For Eastern, Daytona Beach was a stop on its route from

New York to Miami, and its departures from both terminal points were adjusted for the convenience of its passengers. By chance, this resulted in daytime arrivals and departures from Daytona Beach. The bulk of the nation's airmail, however, always had traveled at night, because it is mailed at the close of office hours in the late afternoon.

About two weeks after the Rickenbacker call, Eastern was forced to overfly Daytona Beach because of adverse weather conditions.

Baker wrote a mild letter to Brattain suggesting that, in view of Eastern's inability to serve Daytona Beach properly, Eastern support a petition by National to the Post Office Department for permanent certification by National on the route between Daytona Beach and Jacksonville. If Eastern, however, felt that it could not support this proposal, which was made for the public convenience, then perhaps it could rearrange its schedules so that the Tampa airmail would not be subject to such lengthy delays.

Brattain was remarkably restrained in his reply. ". . . You mentioned that this should not be a difficult problem to solve, but as I see it the only solution you might have to offer is that you continue your flights into Jacksonville. Your route, of course, ends at Daytona Beach, and we can see of no way in which you could expect to extend your operations from Daytona Beach into Jacksonville. . . . Any paralleling of our operation on your part would be objected to by us.

"During the winter we will probably operate two round trips a day through Daytona Beach and set up our schedules so as to go through there during the daytime, when weather conditions are more favorable. I suggest you rearrange your schedules to meet these flights."

A few days later, Baker called upon Jerry Waterman, who, in addition to being a member of the board of National Airlines, was chairman of the aviation committee of the Chamber of Commerce.

If Tampa is to grow as a commercial aviation center, and

it should because of its geographical location, he said, then direct service should be established between here and New Orleans, Kansas City, and Chicago. This should be the focus of attention of the civic groups. I can't bring this before the right people, because we have a personal interest in the outcome of this matter. If Eastern gets Atlanta–Miami via Tampa, it is going to hurt us financially, because they will be paralleling our Tampa–Miami run and everyone will think we have an ulterior motive in bringing up the matter.

Waterman agreed. "Do you have any ideas?" he asked.

Baker clasped his hands behind his head and tipped back in his chair. The Congress convenes November 15, he continued, and there is plenty of time for Mayor Chancey to appoint a non-partisan aviation group to determine which direction is best for Tampa. The recommendations of this group can be forwarded to the Congress, which certainly is going to authorize some new routes, and of course to the Post Office Department, which will implement them. If these new routes are authorized, National of course would bid on them, and so would Eastern and other carriers, but this is unimportant. I'm thinking of the good of the community. If Eastern gets Miami from here, it could put National out of business, and it would leave Tampa and St. Petersburg at the mercy of one carrier. We would be treated in the same shabby manner as they are treating Daytona Beach. If the mayor will name a committee, I'll testify before it. You could testify before it. A good idea would be to invite Rickenbacker to testify before it.

Waterman bought the suggestion and took it to Mayor R. E. L. Chancey, who in turn also thought the idea an excellent one. He named six of the community's leading citizens to the "aviation study group." They were: Carl D. Borein, George B. Howell, E. Preston McGeachy, G. David Curtis, Frank J. Gannon, and Waterman, who was named chairman.

Invitations were sent by the study group to both Rickenbacker and Baker to testify before the group. The appearance was scheduled for November 4. Rickenbacker showed up at noon and went directly to the meeting in the mayor's office. Baker was not present. Waterman explained that National's president had suddenly been called to Washington on urgent business.

"I feel sorry for Tampa," Rickenbacker said. "Progress of this city in aviation has been blocked by selfishness and greed. There is no other explanation." He went on to testify that Tampa needed a major airline, by which it could be connected to the major urban areas of the nation. There was no doubt in the minds of anyone in the room but that the thrust of his remarks was directed toward Baker.

Near the conclusion of his speech, he said, "A line that is fundamentally sound is absolutely necessary. Pan American requires a connecting line that would bring business for the Caribbean and South American area."

A well-dressed man of medium stature in the back of the room stood up when Rickenbacker had finished and asked permission for a question. "As I understand it, you have applied for a route between Atlanta and Miami with an intermediate stop here in Tampa."

Rickenbacker nodded. "That is correct."

"Why don't you terminate your flights here?"

"Because we should connect with Pan American in Miami," Rickenbacker explained.

"But we already have service between here and Miami with National," the man said patiently. He smiled. "I don't want to misrepresent myself," he added. "I'm a stockholder in National and I'm curious as to why you just can't terminate your southbound flights here. National, which is already established on the Miami run, can easily provide connecting service between Pan American and Eastern."

"A major airline is needed," Rickenbacker snapped.

"But National is based right here in St. Petersburg," the man said gently. "Why can't you terminate your flights here and help a local industry?"

Rickenbacker exploded. "Because Tampa is a dead-end town," he roared.

A few hours later, Baker and Lou Bower sat together in the small operations office in St. Petersburg, a newspaper spread out on the desk before them. The headline on page one read:

RICKENBACKER CALLS TAMPA
A DEAD-END TOWN

"I don't know how you did it, Lou," Baker said grinning.

"Well, he has a quick temper," Bower replied.

A few weeks later, the Post Office Department rejected Eastern's bid for a mail route between Atlanta and Miami with an intermediate stop at Tampa. It awarded National Airlines a new route from Jacksonville, Florida, to New Orleans, Louisiana, with intermediate stops at Mobile, Alabama, and Biloxi, Mississippi.

How much influence Rickenbacker's angry remark had upon the decision will never be assessed. Both newspapers, after their first angry reaction, supported Eastern in its bid, but it is known that many irate letters requesting that Eastern be denied the right to serve the Tampa-St. Petersburg area went to congressmen, senators, and the Post Office Department immediately after Rickenbacker's appearance.

According to Robert Foreman, who was secretary of National Airlines for many years, a few days after the award was announced, both Rickenbacker and Brattain showed up unexpectedly in National's offices on the eighth floor of the St. Petersburg Times Building. They asked if they could speak to Baker privately, and the three men left the building. A short time later, Baker returned alone. "Well," he said, "I've just turned down a hell of a lot of money for the airline." Foreman says Baker told him that Rickenbacker then once again had told Baker that he was going to put him out of business.

At this time, National still had not reached a position

where it could pay its bills promptly. It was running between two and three months behind the due dates on all bills. A few weeks after Rickenbacker visited Baker in St. Petersburg, he received a call from the airport saying that the Gulf Oil Corporation had brought out fifty gallons of oil on a C.O.D. basis. Baker sent Foreman out with a check, then angrily called up the local Gulf Oil representative. Not only was the oil on a C.O.D. basis, Baker was told apologetically, but from now on he would have to pay cash for his fuel.

There wasn't enough money in the bank account to keep the planes flying until the next government check arrived, to say nothing of other operating expenses. In desperation, Baker called Standard Oil, expecting to be turned down, but Standard said immediately that there would be no problem with National's credit. The next day Standard was servicing National over its entire system. Years later, after National had been extended into New York and was buying about twelve million gallons of gas a year, a purchasing executive told Baker that he had put the fuel contracts up for bid and that Texaco not only was low bidder, but would supply brand-new ground equipment for the airline as a bonus. "Forget it," Baker replied. "If it wasn't for Standard Oil there wouldn't be an airline. Give them the contract."

Baker was always convinced that Rickenbacker, who also was a customer of Gulf, was responsible for Gulf shutting off his credit. Dave Amos disagrees. "It wasn't that at all," he says. "We just weren't paying our bills." Amos is probably right, because Standard is the basis for the Rockefeller fortune and the Rockefellers had a heavy financial investment in Eastern.

CHAPTER SIX

You do not sell an airline as you sell a house or an automobile or an appliance. One cannot put a classified ad in a newspaper or a trade publication to announce that an airline is for sale. The sale of an airline must be conducted in an aura of secrecy, as is the sale of any large business complex. The reason for this is logical. If it became known to the general public that any big business complex was for sale, the value of the stock would drop, thus dissipating a profit from the sale. The formula is to "put out feelers." A remark is dropped at a cocktail party or a breakfast that "if the price is right, of course the product is for sale." Everything is for sale. It can be said with one inflection at the cocktail party and with another inflection to the financial reporter when he calls to check on the rumor. It is a long and laborious process.

Maytag boarded a flight from Miami to Washington, D.C., and during the flight he estimated that he would need about one year to get rid of Frontier at a reasonable profit. To tie up Baker for this length of time on an option would require a lot of money. The amount of option money to be offered was a delicate area. There is always the psychological factor. If too much is offered, the owner inflates the value of his property. If too little is offered, the owner becomes insulted and indignant, and the deal is lost.

It was most difficult to deal with a person one did not know well. Like Woody, he had heard the stories of how Baker had "taken" Juan Trippe, not once but twice, and Baker's long running feud with Rickenbacker was common knowledge. Baker loved to make deals, and probably he was happiest when he had won a deal or had "taken" someone. It was a game. Quite probably, Trippe and Rickenbacker enjoyed the game with the same gusto as Baker. Things were not the same now as they had been in the helmet-and-goggles days, when this type of game was relatively inexpensive. Still, this was an important point to remember. He should play Baker's game and let Baker think he was winning. Maytag smiled as he realized that, by doing this, he was approaching the problem on the same plane as Baker. He decided he would open by offering Baker two hundred fifty thousand dollars for a one-year option.

When Maytag got off the airplane at Washington National Airport, however, he noticed that the ground equipment for National Airlines was as worn and battered as the terminal building. Then he recalled the paper-covered windows at the airline's general office in Miami. A quarter of a million dollars probably was too much money for an option. Probably one hundred thousand dollars was a more practical figure. This should be a sufficient amount of option money to a man so penurious that he used butcher paper for window shades in his office building. On the other hand, it was a lot of money to lose if he couldn't get rid of Frontier within a year. These thoughts mulled through Maytag's mind as the taxi carried him to the offices of his Washington lawyers.

It seemed that National was always in financial trouble. The original airmail contract guaranteed the equivalent of three hundred pounds of mail at seventeen cents per pound. That amounted to a government subsidy of fifty-one dollars daily so long as the schedules were maintained, a rather modest sum considering that the entire cost of the operation was predicated on the subsidy. In the beginning, when a passenger appeared, the entire staff of the airline was elated. In the entire first year of operation, the airline flew less than four hundred passengers, with a total revenue from passenger income of less than five thousand dollars. It took about the same amount of money to keep the planes in an airworthy condition. The two Ryans were secondhand before the airline was started, and there were several forced landings.

Horton Hale landed one on the back of a cow near Orlando. On the following day, Kershaw, in the other Ryan, lost a propeller near Daytona Beach. Three days' subsidy was lost before the two-plane fleet became operational again. A short time later, Kershaw took off from St. Petersburg with two male passengers whose instant dislike for each other erupted into a wild, slugging melee. Kershaw, ducking the flailing fists, managed to land the Ryan in a field, again near Orlando, and push his fighting passengers out of the aircraft. Before he could take off, one of the sluggers swung a punch that lifted his opponent from the ground and drove him through the fabric-covered fuselage of the aircraft. Again, flights were forced to cancel.

By early 1936 Baker realized that he could not run his airline much longer with a fleet of two antiquated Ryans. Not only was the equipment falling apart, but he still was nervous over the threatened competition from Gulf. It was at this time that he borrowed the money from Harry Parker that financed the purchase of the Stinsons from Western Airlines, with enough money left over to make the down payment on a new, ten-passenger Lockheed Electra.

One of the Ryans was sold as soon as the first Stinson arrived. Its purchaser was a Mexican general whose pilot demolished it while ferrying it to Chihuahua, where the general was waiting. The pilot, who escaped with minor injuries, claimed Baker had misrepresented the plane's capabilities to him, and the general sued Baker, seeking the return of his money. No record can be found today as to the final outcome of the suit.

Baker's money problems were not unique. Many of the

other carriers were having financial problems, but National, unlike many of the other carriers, had never experienced an airmail subsidy that was sufficiently large so as to be considered a comfortable financial cushion. When the carrying of the airmail was restored to competitive bidding by the passage of the Black Act, the postal subsidy payments rarely equaled operational costs. Thus profits were predicated upon passengers, and all the airlines fought for these brave souls with the vigor of tomcats seeking control of a harem. Baker came up with the idea of a space-available annual pass for local politicians and civic leaders, which required a two-dollar service charge, and the monies collected from these often meant the difference between meeting a payroll and not. His action was typical of the wild price-cutting war being waged for passenger traffic by the forty-four subsidized and unsubsidized air carriers in existence at the time of the National-Gulf merger.

The potential passenger market was not increasing to any noticeable degree, because of the number of crashes and the attendant publicity. The larger subsidized carriers realized that, if they were to survive, they must cease clawing each other and work in certain areas as a cohesive unit. The result was the formation of an industry-wide organization known as the Air Transport Association. Baker's first reaction toward joining the ATA was negative. It "smacked too much of unionism," but eventually he signed up.

The strategy of the Air Transport Association apparently was to seek stronger regulations from the federal government in order to push the weaker, non-member carriers out of business. The ATA president invited the government to move in.

"Of the $120,000,000 of private investment which has been made in American air transportation, more than half is gone. This condition of financial starvation not only makes it impossible for these lines to take advantage of possible technological improvements, but could lead to traffic competition of such intensity that the accident ratio might accelerate instead of decline. Failure to correct the existing situation and to do so promptly means more than loss to the capital remaining invested in the air transport industry, to the labor employed in it, and to this country's position in civil aviation. It may well entail a large cost in human life."

The invitation sparked a plethora of aviation bills in the Congress. Spokesmen for the State, War, Post Office, and Commerce departments each suggested that his department was best qualified to regulate the aviation industry. Regulatory agencies that had been born under the Roosevelt administration also clamored for control. Roosevelt was forced to act quickly. The virtual ultimatum from the Air Transport Association implied that, if there were another fatal crash, it would be the fault of the government, and the memory of the Air Corps fiasco in carrying the mail was still too recent for the public to put away as history. The President appointed a committee consisting of a representative from each competing bureau, department, agency, and commission seeking control of the aviation industry. This committee eventually decided that control should be vested in either the Interstate Commerce Commission or in a new agency to be set up by Congress. The new-agency idea was chosen, and the result was the passage by Congress of the Civil Aeronautics Act of 1938. The Act created a Civil Aeronautics Authority, with the power to regulate both the economic and safety conditions of the airline industry within the United States. A short time later, in keeping with the times, the Civil Aeronautics Authority was split into two parts, with a separate economic regulatory unit, consisting of five political appointees, known as the Civil Aeronautics Board. Many years later, the CAA became the Federal Aviation Agency.

The passage of the Act was welcomed delightedly by the airlines. It protected their existing routes and almost eliminated the threat of outside competition. More important from the airlines' point of view, the Act provided that carriage of airmail would no longer be on a contract basis subject to competitive bids. Mail pay now was to be awarded to a carrier on the basis of "need." Not only would the existing nineteen trunk-line carriers no longer face any losses, but they also were guaranteed a reasonable return on their investment. It was a guaranteed annual income.

Yet it is unlikely that there is any airline president today who has not damned the CAB upon more than one occasion. On the other hand, it is equally unlikely that there is any president who would welcome the dissolution of the CAB despite continuing criticism of the Board. Maytag was once asked this question at a press conference.

"I think all of us at some time or another find ourselves in disagreement with some policies of the Board," he replied. "But I shudder to think of the situations that would arise if there were no such regulatory agency."

Baker reacted quickly to the passage of the Act. He bought another secondhand Stinson and two more Lockheed Electras and sold the remaining Ryan. At the same time, he filed a brief before the newly instituted Civil Aeronautics Board. National had been flying two separate and unconnected routes. Planes used on the Jacksonville–New Orleans segment had to be ferried to St. Petersburg for maintenance, a costly procedure. On one occasion, a Stinson was grounded in Jacksonville for want of a small part. It was flown by National to Daytona Beach, where it was placed on an Eastern plane to be picked up in Jacksonville. The shipment was misplaced. A replacement was again flown to Daytona Beach and shipped north by train. The Stinson was out of service for three days.

In his petition before the Board, Baker asked that National be certified to fly between Daytona Beach and Jacksonville, and he used as an argument one that still is being used today by regional carriers seeking route extensions. By closing the gap between the two routes, the federal government could reduce the subsidy payments and thus benefit the taxpayer. The case was the first to be argued before the Civil Aeronautics Board.

Eastern Airlines, predictably, was upset over the petition, and it responded in a manner that set a precedent that still is followed to a lesser degree in all route cases before the Board. It sought endorsement of its opposition to the National extension from civic groups, municipalities, chambers of commerce, and as many politicians as it could garner.

At this time, John L. Morris was working for the Miami Chamber of Commerce. A soft-spoken southern gentleman, he had for many years been an editor of the Tampa *Tribune,* then general manager of the Chamber of Commerce in Macon, Georgia. He had met Baker socially on two or three occasions because of mutual aviation interests, and presently was exploring the possibility of Baker's moving National's general offices to Miami. The day before the hearings opened in the Carlton Hotel, Morris was in Washington on other business. He received a telephone call from John Hall, the president of the Miami Chamber, asking him to testify in the case on behalf of Miami.

"I'm not sure I know enough about it to testify," Morris replied.

"Go see Smythe Gambrell, and he will fill you in."

Gambrell was general counsel for Eastern. Morris found him at the Carlton Hotel. Gambrell was cordial, but rushed. He gave Morris some papers explaining Eastern's position. "All you have to say really," he added, "is that the Miami Chamber endorses Eastern's stand. You understand that, if there is competition, Eastern may be forced to curtail some of its flights into Miami."

When the hearings opened, Chief Examiner Francis Brown sat at the top of an immense T-shaped table. On one side of the stem sat a score of attorneys appearing on behalf of Eastern and Rickenbacker. On the other side of the long table were three men: Ted Baker, Bill Denning, and John Cross, the latter two attorneys for National. Denning was a "country-style" lawyer, and there were many who saw a resemblance in his casual-style dress to the gallus-snapping criminal attorney Clarence Darrow. Denning, however, was an expert in the intricacies of Washington regulatory agencies, having specialized in practice for several years before the Interstate Commerce Commission. He was as familiar with Baker as he was with the newly formed Civil Aeronautics Board. Less than a month earlier, Baker had appeared unannounced in Denning's office, asked the attorney to have lunch with him, and when the invitation was declined because of a previous engagement, retained Denning to represent National. Denning remained Baker's Washington attorney until he retired from practice many years later. John Cross was a short, stocky, crew-cut young man "who looked more like a kid out of college" than a practicing legal associate of Denning. John Morris thought that National did not have much of a chance of winning the case with such a battery of talent aligned against it.

When Morris finally was called to the stand, by Gambrell, he testified only that the Greater Miami area needed all the air service it could get. He mentioned neither Eastern nor National.

When he was finished, Denning asked him one question. "Are you testifying on behalf of Eastern Airlines?"

Morris shook his head. "I am testifying on behalf of Miami and its air-service needs."

Denning thanked him. Gambrell looked thoughtful.

A couple of days later, when Morris was back in Miami, he received a long-distance call from Baker thanking him for the manner in which he had testified.

"I testified for what I thought best for Miami," Morris replied. "I showed no partiality for either Eastern or National."

"I know," Baker replied, than abruptly changed the subject. "I have decided that Miami is the best location for our general offices. Would Miami be sufficiently interested in having us to pay for all of the cost of moving and other considerations?"

Miami was indeed interested. Morris visited most of the city and county officials, and after a few meetings and a few weeks, obtained the commitment Baker wanted. Morris personally flew to St. Petersburg with the official presentation and found Baker highly elated. He had just received word from the CAB that his certificate between Daytona Beach and Jacksonville had been granted, with an effective date of March 21, 1940. Baker also was pleased by the proposal from Miami. "The move just needs the formality of approval from the board of directors," he said.

Morris returned to Miami and reported the apparent success of his mission. A few weeks later, he opened a copy of the morning Miami *Herald* and read that National Airlines was moving its headquarters from St. Petersburg to Jacksonville. He called Baker.

"Yeah, that's right," Baker said. "They're not only going to move us, but they're going to build us a hangar." He paused. "I might be able to kill the deal if you'll build us a hangar and an office building."

Morris swore silently and hung up. "At that time, if anyone had told me that six years later Baker would offer me a job and that I would accept, I would have called him an absolute fool," Morris says. Yet shortly after the end of World War II, Baker bumped into Morris in the Carlton Hotel in Washington and did offer him a job at a salary attractive enough for Morris to accept.

Shortly after the move to Jacksonville, Baker once again was approached by Rickenbacker, who offered to buy National, and once again Baker refused. But after this offer was made, Baker approached C. R. Woolman, the president and founder of Delta Airlines, and proposed that Delta buy out National. There are several stories that this proposed merger fell through because of Baker's insistence that he be made chairman of Delta's board, and that Woolman would not have any part of Baker in his company.

John Cross says, however, that the proposed marriage fell through purely because of a matter of price. National was offered for sale, and Woolman offered one price and Baker wanted another. The two men dickered for many months but could not reach an agreement despite the fact that they were only twenty-five cents a share apart on price. Woolman offered 7¼. Baker demanded 7½.

CHAPTER SEVEN

The question of the possibility of illegality in tendering an option to purchase control of an airline was settled quickly in Washington, and Maytag returned to Denver. There were no prohibitions on an option offer, and an option document was drawn by John Love, a Colorado Springs attorney and long-time friend of Maytag who later became governor of Colorado.

Maytag moved slowly and methodically, because timing was the most delicate part of the negotiation. If he moved too quickly, he would appear too eager and the premium on the price of the controlling shares would soar. Conversely, Maytag knew that if he delayed too long, there was the possibility that Baker might sell to someone else or merge with another carrier. All the trunk carriers were going through an era of jet indigestion. American and Eastern were seeking permission from the Civil Aeronautics Board to merge. Capitol Airlines had been swallowed by United, and Northeast had had most of its fleet repossessed. The feelers put out for the sale of Frontier were not attracting worth-while attention.

National was making money, but not as much as Maytag and Woody thought it should. Part of the problem was the shortage of jet equipment. When the Southern Transcontinental Route award was made to National, Baker operated only three jet aircraft. These were medium-range DC-8s of early vintage. He had on order three DC-8 fan jets and had arranged to lease from Douglas three more. While awaiting delivery of these, he had temporarily leased the first DC-8 prototype, thus giving him a total of only four jet aircraft to operate over the system. San Francisco and San Diego had no jet service. The traffic was carried by Lockheed Electras, and for many weeks, because of a series of accidents caused under certain conditions by oscillation of the engines in their mountings, they were restricted to a slow speed by the Federal Aviation Authority until they could be modified.

The first visit by Maytag to Baker occurred in mid-July. Maytag made his second trip to Miami shortly after Labor Day, and again he met with Baker in his office. Baker's attitude had changed perceptibly. He seemed suspicious of his visitor, and every time Maytag brought up the reason for his visit, Baker would only listen and make no reply. Sometimes he spun around in his chair to avoid an answer. On other occasions, he changed the subject, discussing some trivial aspect of the airline industry. Baker was indecisive. After a long while, Baker abruptly asked Maytag if he knew Rickenbacker.

"I know of him, but I have never met him."

"Who do you know at Eastern?"

Maytag suddenly realized what was going through Baker's mind. He was afraid that Maytag was acting on behalf of some other carrier, that Maytag might be buying National only to turn around and sell it to someone else. It did not make sense. Either the carrier was for sale or it was not for sale. If it was for sale, what difference did it make who bought it, providing the price was agreed upon? "So far as I am concerned, no one at Eastern, or any other carrier, knows that I am here," he said aloud.

Baker appeared unconvinced.

Later, Maytag called Ray Woody in Denver. "I don't know whether we're going to make a deal or not," he commented. "You were sure right when you said this guy was difficult to deal with."

Another thought kept occurring to Maytag. He wanted to

stay in the airline business, and he had to sell Frontier before he could buy National. If he sold Frontier, however, and then found that Baker would not sell National, he would be out of the business. It was one hell of a gamble, but he decided to still keep the feelers out for the sale of Frontier. After all, Baker had indicated earlier that he would sell.

After the merger with Gulf and the resulting incorporation, Baker addressed the problem of financing the carrier.

"He felt he had something tangible to sell," Bower says. "I don't think he felt that he was selling a portion of a two-bit airline. The airline was his own property forever. No one else ever owned one nut or one bolt of it. What he was selling was paper, gilt-edged paper stock certificates, and although he raised money by the sale of stock, I think he always believed that he had been gypped when the stock increased in value."

Bower bought some of the stock at one dollar a share and some more at a dollar fifty. In connection with one block of five thousand shares that was sold to Bower, Baker wrote the following letter.

> Dear Lou:
> Confirming our conversation of yesterday I will be glad to sell you five thousand shares of the capital stock of this company, provided, of course, that I keep the stock in my possession, or can obtain the same from you (when needed) from your account. . . . I am to have voting power of the stock until such time as you desire to dispose of it and I am to have the first option to purchase same at your cost price. . . .

Bower bought the stock. Many years later, when the same five thousand shares were worth more than one hundred thousand dollars, Baker reminded Bower that he still had the right to buy it back for five thousand dollars.

Other blocks of stock were sold to Harry Parker of the

Flash-Tric Electric Sign Company in Chicago, but the price Parker paid for it is unknown. There is speculation that the transaction retired a fifteen-thousand-dollar debt owed by Baker to Parker. About this same time, Harry Parker, Jr., was named a vice president of National, an appointment that Bower says was related directly to the stock purchase by the senior Parker.

There is another story that the senior Parker also lent Baker $25,000 for operating capital at the same time he purchased the stock. According to Robert Foreman, "Baker went to Chicago and came back with five $5000 checks from Parker. Baker kept these checks in his desk. When he got clear out of money, he would deposit one check for $5000 in the bank. He made that money last for a year and a half."

Foreman adds that the money was repaid without interest in 1942.

Another financial break for National came from Lehman Brothers, the prominent New York banking firm. Shortly after National was extended into New Orleans from Jacksonville, Baker met a New Orleans stockbroker named Norvin Harris at a social function. Harris was a close friend of Joseph A. Thomas, a partner in the Lehman Brothers firm, and it was Harris who arranged for Baker and Thomas to meet in New York. As a result of that meeting, twenty thousand shares were subscribed to by the banking firm.

There have been many reports that the stock was sold for two fifty a share, although it had an equity value of only thirteen cents. According to *Fortune* magazine, this subscription came under investigation by the Civil Aeronautics Board, but this is unlikely, as the CAB was not in existence when the stock was floated. There is no apparent record of any investigation by the Civil Aeronautics Board at a later date, and Thomas can recall no investigation of the transaction by any government agency.

Thomas, who is regarded as one of the top half-dozen most influential people on Wall Street, also questions the equity value of thirteen cents. "I'm surprised it was that high. The equity value was based upon the romantic hopes for the airline at that time."

The financier says that Lehman Brothers actually did not underwrite the issue of twenty thousand shares. "It was a group of Lehman Brothers employees who bought the shares. We were placing a bet on some guy to develop an airline. It's what we in the banking business call a crap shot—or like placing a bet at the two-dollar window at Aqueduct."

Thomas says that this occurred during the days when the airlines still had a romantic appeal—when a guy would quit a fifty-dollar-a-week job to go to work for an airline at thirty dollars a week.

Thomas and Baker became close friends, and for several years Thomas served on National's board of directors. When he resigned in the mid-fifties, he was still retained by Baker as a financial consultant.

Thus, by the start of World War II, Baker had his hands on at least a hundred fifty thousand dollars, which was far short of his goal of a million at forty, but it probably would have bought as much as a million would today. He also had control of an airline that ran up both coasts of Florida and as far west as New Orleans.

World War II provided the impetus for National's greatest growth. Had it not been for the war, National probably would have remained a small carrier that long ago would have been absorbed by one of the giants. Much has been written about Baker's great coups, such as the leasing of jets from Pan American to start the first jet operations in the United States. Nothing, however, can exceed his delicate use of the military to expand National from a minor regional carrier into a trunk that by war's end had routes extending as far north as New York. Then, although the momentum of expansion was slowing down, there was sufficient force to move the route expansion north to Boston and south into Havana, making National an international carrier.

One of Baker's former executives once said, "Ted's a great guy until you go to work for him. Then he gets mad, because he thinks you are taking money away from him."

There is a strong element of truth in this. There was no life in a corporate crystal palace when Baker was around. In some ways he was extraordinarily penurious. He would personally scrutinize the long-distance phone calls made by his officers, and he would promote and demote them so that they bounced up and down as if on the end of a yo-yo string. There were a few exceptions, such as Lew Dymond, his vice president of flight operations and later president of Frontier Airlines, but most of his officers did not know from one day to the next their status in the company. At one time he had a vice president of sales and traffic to whom he was paying eighteen thousand dollars a year. Reporting to him was an assistant vice president of sales who was being paid thirty thousand dollars.

In the formative years of the airline, this erratic wage schedule continued down to the lowest echelon, and so, as the airline began to grow, the unions found a large percentage of National's employees most agreeable to membership. Reservations clerks, ticket agents, mechanics, even stewardesses, organized into several unions, and Baker fought them all bitterly.

It was inevitable that these hostilities and resentments would break out into the open, and the fight was triggered by an incident that occurred in Tampa on September 13, 1945.

The weather was bad. There were many thunderstorms in the area, and the Lodestar pilot, coming in for a landing, noticed a squall sweeping toward the airport shortly before he was ready to touch down. He retracted the landing gear and went around the airport. On his second approach he came in too high, and once again he was forced to go around the airport. On his third approach ground radio personnel heard him say, "Well, I've missed it twice; I'll be damned if I'm going to miss it a third time." He wasn't damned, because he did get the wheels on the runway, but he was so close to the end of it that he was forced to ground-loop the aircraft. When it finally came to a stop, its nose was hanging on a sea wall and the rest of the plane was under the water of Tampa Bay. No one was injured, but the passengers had to climb out the cockpit window, and the aircraft was demolished.

Baker promptly, and justifiably, fired the pilot. It was Baker's contention that the pilot was incompetent and that he was fired, not because he had destroyed an airplane, but because his lack of judgment might result in a more serious accident in the future. Baker was sincere in his conviction. The accusations that he was furious because he had lost an airplane do not hold up. Earlier, E. J. Kershaw had belly-landed a Lodestar at Jacksonville because of a mechanical problem with the landing gear. The plane had been torn apart badly, but Baker had given Kershaw a cash bonus and a raise because of the skillful manner in which he had handled the emergency.

The pilots, by this time, had been organized into the Air Line Pilots Association, and the discharged pilot promptly filed what is known as a grievance over his termination. The agreement between ALPA and the airline at this time called for the formation of a committee consisting of two members of ALPA and two members of the company. If this equally divided partisan board was unable to reach an agreement, then the board would lose jurisdiction, and, in effect, the case would blow away. It was almost tantamount to a ruling against the employee. He would remain discharged.

In this case the board divided evenly, ALPA backing its member and the management representatives backing the company. The case, however, did not blow away. Despite the language of the agreement, ALPA insisted that the discharged pilot be reinstated. It was not a matter for quick resolution, with ALPA consistently raising the threat of a strike.

Eventually, the dispute was referred to the National Mediation Board under the appropriate section of the Railway

Labor Act. In its attempt to solve the problem, the NMB finally prevailed upon an obdurate Baker to agree to the appointment of a neutral to hear the case. Again time passed as both the airline and ALPA tried to agree upon a neutral. When this became deadlocked, the NMB stepped in and appointed Oscar Baake as the neutral board member. Baake was a staff member of the Civil Aeronautics Authority, in the department of the CAA that concerned itself primarily with airline accidents. Baake was an expert in the field and was eminently qualified in terms of being void of partiality, but Baake's appointment was strongly protested by David Behncke, the founding president of ALPA.

Behncke wrote a long letter to the National Mediation Board objecting to the appointment of Baake, and the NMB then asked Baake to turn down the appointment—which he did. The NMB then appointed a prominent Texas attorney to whom Baker objected, not so much on the grounds that the lawyer was biased as that ALPA had torpedoed the appointment of Baake.

While all this was going on, Baker also was having trouble with the International Association of Machinists, which represented both the station workers and the clerical employees. One of the prime issues in the dispute was the continued right of the airline to farm out to contractors the loading and unloading of its aircraft. With the clerical workers, it was purely a matter of higher salaries. In January of 1948 the IAM struck the airline.

Baker reluctantly started to back off. He asked Kershaw to call ALPA to tell them National would settle the pilots' dispute on their terms. Today, apparently, no one remembers whom Kershaw called at ALPA other than that it was not Dave Behncke.

The answer from the unknown spokesman for ALPA is remembered. "I'm sorry, but you have too many other labor problems."

Baker's reply was succinct. "Screw 'em," he said. "If I can't settle the thing on their own terms, let them go."

On February 3, 1948, the pilots struck. No notice was given. At a given time, system-wide, they walked out of their airplanes. Some of the planes were even loaded with passengers. Three DC-4s were left at Newark in fifty-minute parking gates. The aircraft were abandoned at cities all over the system. The pilots returned to Miami by train, bus, and other carriers, even abandoning the stewardesses.

Supervisory personnel, such as "Skeeter" Royall, now the airline's chief pilot; Steve Wedge, now vice president of flight operations; Wally Fordyce, Gene Modell, and others, immediately left Miami to pick up the abandoned aircraft and stewardesses.

"We landed in every place where we had an employee stranded," Wedge recalls, "and dropped them off on the way home. We brought the airplanes into Miami, and many of the striking pilots were out to greet us, waving signs and calling us scabs and bastards and other similar endearing terms.

"Also on hand to greet us was Baker, and this is the only time in my life I ever saw him emotionally triggered. He picked us up himself, and he actually had tears in his eyes. 'The die is cast now,' he said. 'We're just going to hire a bunch of new pilots, and we'll rebuild this goddam airline right from scratch.'"

At this time there was a large reservoir of war-surplus pilots in the country, all of them good fliers who required a minimum of training for transition to the airline's equipment. In less than a week, service was partially resumed. Within five months, the airline was back in full operation.

It was a bitter strike. The pilots who were flying were harassed constantly. Telephone calls were made to their homes incessantly. The pilots were cursed at every stop, and there were numerous fist fights. A ground-school instructor for the new pilots was murdered. His assailant was never caught, and there is no way of knowing whether the murder was related to the strike. The striking pilots printed thousands of match packets urging the public not to fly National, and distributed them throughout the United States. They even picketed by air, forming a flying "squadron" that cruised up and down the East Coast. They concentrated on cities served by National, and as one group called upon the mayor and other civic leaders seeking their support in the National boycott, another group would fly rented planes over the city towing large streamers that said, "Don't Fly National." The flying squadron played tag with Morris, who was covering the same cities seeking endorsement of National's position. On one occasion the two narrowly missed each other in Charleston, South Carolina. When Morris came out of the mayor's office, he passed two members of ALPA waiting in the anteroom. Both were reading magazines and did not notice Morris.

Typical of the time was an experience of Lew Dymond, who then was assistant operations manager for National:

"We came into Jacksonville in a DC-4. I was not flying the trip although everyone on the picket line thought I was one of the pilots. The picket line extended from about two and one half to three blocks, from above the terminal building to the hangar. It was packed from about six to eight feet deep with our employees and their friends and relatives.

"I had gone up to Jacksonville to see if I could smooth things down a bit, and I was the last person to get off the airplane. As I walked through the picket line someone spit on me, and at the same time someone kicked me in the rear. I turned around quickly enough to see that it was one of our striking pilots who had kicked me, so I slugged him. About that time, four of the pilots jumped on my back and down we went.

"There were about thirty policemen around, and four of them picked me up, two cops on each arm. Four more picked up the pilot, and they threw us both in the back end of a prowl car. Then another pilot named Bob Peck, who has since died, put his head in the car and said, 'Officer, you look after that Dymond guy. He is a no-good son of a bitch.' I leaned over to say something to him, and I crunched down on the pilot's instep, and then we were going at it again in the back seat of the car."

Both Dymond and the pilot were taken to the Jacksonville jail. Dymond fortunately was carrying enough money with him to post bail. The pilot remained in the jail overnight until the union could bail him out the following morning.

A few days after the pilots struck, Baker requested the National Mediation Board to recommend to President Truman that a strike had occurred that threatened interstate commerce. Under the language of the Railway Labor Act, the President had the power to appoint an emergency board that hopefully could bring about a resolution to the dispute. The National Mediation Board, however, ruled that the strike against the airline did not affect interstate commerce and thus the creation of an emergency board was unwarranted.

By June of 1948, however, the picture had changed. National was in full operation. Its scheduling was back to normal and its load factors were good despite the fact that it was struck by both the IAM and ALPA. It was then that ALPA began pressing for the creation of an emergency board, and in order to support its stand that the strike was a threat to interstate commerce, the union indicated that its members would not fly into any airport that was being served by National and its strikebreaking pilots.

At this time there was another struggle going on in the country that was much greater in scope than the fight between Baker and the unions. It was an election year, the year in which the polls were unanimous in their opinion that the incumbent Harry Truman would be replaced by the Republican Thomas Dewey. The Democratic administration understandably was extremely susceptible to any suggestions made by any facet of organized labor, from which its greatest support stemmed. Thus, using the "hot airport deal" as an excuse, the National Mediation Board, in June, created an emergency board to look into the dispute.

At one of the early meetings of the emergency board, the question was raised as to whether ALPA would respect the IAM picket line around the airline if the dispute between ALPA and National were resolved. Spokesmen for ALPA replied that the pilots would cross the picket line if the dispute were settled.

It was a complete about-face. The dispute had arisen over the discharge of an allegedly incompetent pilot. Then the pilots had refused to accept a settlement of this dispute on their own terms, because the airline "had too many labor problems," which can only be construed as complete support of the IAM. Now this support, which was the basis of the walkout, was kissed off as unimportant.

When word of this reached the IAM, it retaliated by resuming negotiations with National, and it was generally accepted that as soon "as some minor details were ironed out and the new contract signed," the members of the IAM would cheerfully cross the pilots' picket line on their way to and from work.

Baker was in no hurry to settle any labor dispute, although he was losing money heavily. He believed it extremely unlikely that the pilots for the other twelve trunk carriers would invoke the "hot airport deal." He also objected strenuously to the giving up by the airline of the right to decide whether or not a captain was or was not a good pilot. The negotiations before the emergency board dragged slowly through the summer.

Dewey was nominated by the Republicans for the presidency; Truman was nominated to oppose him.

The next step in the sequence of events admittedly is speculative but is generally accepted as fact within the airline industry. No one thought Truman had the slightest chance to beat Dewey. The polls and the pundits had all given the election to the Republican candidate. Truman knew that he could emerge victorious only with the undivided support of the powerful AF of L and CIO labor organizations. ALPA was a part of the AF of L. The power of ALPA was being seriously threatened by the successful strikebreaking operation of Ted Baker of National Airlines.

It was a trade. The incumbent Democrats needed labor support, and labor, in the form of ALPA, needed federal support to maintain the cohesiveness of their union. In return for undivided labor support, the Truman Administration gave ALPA what is known as Docket 3500.

In 1948 there were many provisions in the law for the benefit of workers of merged companies. If National could be forced to merge, then the strike would be settled, as the pilots would go back to work in the surviving airline.

On September 28, 1948, a little more than a month before the national elections, the Civil Aeronautics Board set down on its agenda Docket 3500, the National Airlines Dismemberment Case. The Board ordered an investigation to determine whether or not it would be in the public interest to transfer "upon just and reasonable terms and conditions, the authorizations and equipment and other property of National Airlines, Inc." to certain named carriers. The beneficiaries of National's death proposed by the CAB would be Pan American, Delta, and Eastern. Other carriers immediately applied for portions of National's route structure.

The announced reason for the proposed dismemberment was that National's precarious financial position warranted such action.

Jerry Waterman says that it was about this time that Eastern once again moved against National. "There was about $250,000 in outstanding loans from several banks. Laurance Rockefeller went to some of these banks and offered to buy these notes."

Because of his connection with Eastern, Waterman believes, if Rockefeller's offer had been accepted, the notes would immediately have been called in for payment. National did not have enough money to meet them, and it would have been shut down even before a death sentence could be imposed by the CAB.

"A member of the board of directors of one of the banks here which had loaned money to National was a Mr. Puckett, who also was president of Allied Stores," Waterman says. "Mr. Puckett told the bank board of directors that Mr. Baker was fighting a fight for all of us because he was being held up by the unions and that he would be put out of business if we sold his notes. He said if the Rockefeller offer was accepted, he would resign as a director of the bank. The board decided not to sell the notes to Mr. Rockefeller and allowed Mr. Baker to pay them later when he was in better shape."

The CAB made one oversight in its proposal to split up National. It mentioned all of National's routes except the one between Miami and Key West.

"Well, maybe the Board doesn't really want to put us all the way out of business after all," Baker told a Miami reporter. "Perhaps the five-member Board will permit us to keep operating between Miami and Key West with our fleet of four 53-passenger DC-6s, seven 46-passenger DC-4s, and twelve 14-passenger Lodestars.

"Let's see; it's less than an hour's flight each way, and with about ten hours' operation of each plane daily, we could handle about seventy-five hundred passengers every day between the two points."

Privately, however, Baker was not joking. "That sonofabitch not only destroyed an airplane. It looks like he has blown up the whole airline," he said.

CHAPTER EIGHT

At the annual meeting of the board of directors and the stockholders in November of 1961, Baker was re-elected president and chairman of the board, which had been expected. Because he held these two top positions, he also was chief executive officer. Immediately after the election, however, Baker made a move that was completely unexpected. He resigned as president and asked the board to elect his nephew, Robert E. Weiland, to the vacancy. At the time, Weiland held the position of vice president in charge of National's northern region.

One officer and member of the board, a long-time associate of Baker, literally was stunned when he heard the announcement. He had been with National for many years, and he was convinced that he would be the one to succeed Baker as president. He rose half out of his seat with his mouth open, then slowly sat down, hands clenching the arms of his chair, staring at Baker in sheer disbelief.

In Denver, Colorado, Bud Maytag also reacted to the news, but in a more thoughtful manner. If Baker was partially retiring, it could be an indication that something was brewing. The article in the local paper was too brief to be informative. It did not explain, for example, who was to be the chief executive officer. If Baker still held this position, then Baker still was running the airline. If Weiland assumed this position, then it meant that Baker indeed was planning to take it easy, live off his income from dividends possibly, and that he had no intention of selling the carrier.

The next day's edition of *The Wall Street Journal* carried the story in more detail, and it stated that no National Airlines official would comment as to the identity of the chief executive officer. Maytag called Baker in Miami and found him as friendly as a used-car salesman before a sale. "I've been reading about you in the papers," Maytag said.

"Yeah, we're moving things around a little."

"Who's the chief executive officer?" Maytag asked bluntly.

Baker laughed. "There wasn't any action taken on that."

Maytag smiled. Baker still was running the airline. "I'm still willing to pay your ridiculous price for it," he said aloud.

"Let me know when you are ready."

"I'll give you an option any time."

"No. You come to me without any CAB problems, and then we'll talk."

Maytag was thoughtful as he replaced the receiver in its cradle. There surely was a reason for naming Weiland as president. He shrugged. The answer would be forthcoming eventually. There were two other problems of more immediate concern than the maneuvers of the unpredictable Baker. Frontier had to be sold, and he had to figure out how he was going to raise the necessary capital to buy control of National "without hocking the family jewels."

On either the same night or the night following the call from Maytag, Baker held a small dinner party in his Miami home at Bay Point. Among those present were Lou Bower and Lew Dymond.

"After dinner he told me and Lew that he had taken a hundred-thousand-dollar option check on a deal involving National that would make him a multimillionaire," Bower says. "I asked him to take my stock in with him, but he said he couldn't do it. Then he said he didn't know whether the deal would go through, because the principal was involved in another airline, and that he had to get rid of it before he could make a move. It was said in such a casual manner that it was accepted casually and I didn't really think a hell of a lot about it. I remember he said he'd probably have sold the whole airline for a hundred thousand dollars if the offer had been made right after the dismemberment case was instigated."

Although Baker had been offered a hundred thousand dollars by Maytag, he had refused it. No one ever will know why Baker told this story, but it played a decisive role in Dymond's actions a few months later.

Although Baker was convinced that the dismemberment proceedings had been instigated by the striking pilots, he quickly became aware that they had powerful political allies who were motivated by the pending division of the spoils. The strongest supporter of the dismemberment case, Baker suspected, was Juan Trippe, of Pan American, who had well demonstrated his political adroitness, not only in the United States, but around the world, and Baker was well aware of the legend that Trippe had even toppled governments in Latin America in order to obtain routes for Pan Am. One thing Trippe never had been able to accomplish, however, was a route within the United States, and the domestic route he coveted the most was the one between Miami and New York. Such a route would link Pan American's North Atlantic operations, headquartered in New York, with the carrier's Latin American operations, headquartered in Miami. When Baker saw that Pan American was in on the spoils, he realized that he was fighting on two fronts in his battle to survive. If the dismemberment case was merely pressure from the pilots to settle the strike, the docket could be dismissed quickly by settling the strike.

This was the less important of the two battles, as was evidenced by the fact that he did settle the dispute with the pilots less than two months after Docket 3500 was placed on the CAB agenda. The fact that it took this long was a matter of face saving. The pilots wanted to get back on the payroll and Baker wanted them back, and so the negotiations went smoothly and quickly.

Either Baker had expert advice or he had a talent for corporate political machination that he never had exhibited before. It is also possible that he adopted the attitude that it is better to have a small percentage of something than 100% of nothing.

Bower thinks differently. "There was nothing Ted enjoyed more than a good fight," he says. "In this case it was a fight with different weapons; that's all."

In order to understand Baker's moves, it is necessary to take a brief look at Pan American's route structure in South America. Pan Am had the rights as an American-flag carrier to fly from Miami to Panamá and then on down the eastern coast of South America to Buenos Aires. Some years earlier, Pan Am had gone into a fifty-fifty partnership with W. R. Grace, of the Grace Steamship Lines, to form Panagra Air Lines, which secured route authority down the western coast of South America to Santiago, Chile, and then across the Andes to Buenos Aires. The northern terminal point for Panagra was Panamá.

For years, Grace and Trippe had been feuding with the same vigor as Rickenbacker and Baker, because Grace wished to extend Panagra up into the United States but was blocked from so doing by Trippe. Because each owned 50% of the carrier, the dispute was a stalemate.

Baker cannily decided to play Grace and Trippe against each other as a solution to his dilemma with the CAB. He first proposed to both Grace and Trippe that National fly Panagra's planes between New York and Miami. Pan Am could then fly the Panagra plane on to Panamá, where it could connect with Panagra's route structure. Grace immediately accepted the proposal. Trippe was unimpressed. He had a very good chance of getting the New York–Miami run after National's demise, and apparently he saw no point in letting Panagra get even a minor foothold within the United States.

Baker next met with Peter Grace, a descendant of W. R. Grace and Panagra president, and sold him 174,000 shares of National stock at five fifty a share, which was a dollar and a half below the market price. Although the transaction had to be approved by the Civil Aeronautics Board, it changed the whole concept of the National dismemberment case, and Trippe was understandably furious. If Panagra were allowed to become a major stockholder in National, then there would be a strong possibility that Panagra would win the coveted New York–Miami segment of National's route. Then it would be only a matter of time before the CAB allowed Panagra to link its route by extending it from Miami to Panamá.

Before Trippe could take any remedial action, Baker increased the pressure. After a meeting of the Air Transport Association in Washington, which he attended, he hinted to an aviation writer that the Panagra transaction was but the first step in a plan to have Panagra take over the entire National system. The proposal, he indicated, would be submitted to National stockholders with the recommendation that it be accepted as the best solution to Docket 3500. If this was approved, Baker pointed out, it could eventually give Panagra direct access to South America from all the cities in National's system.

Trippe immediately met with Baker, and in an extraordinarily brief session, Baker obligingly agreed to give Trippe an option on 30% of National's stock, which if exercised, would make Pan American the majority stockholder in National.

Any feeling of well-being that Trippe may have felt over this coup was short-lived. He barely had time for a good night's sleep when he learned that Baker had optioned another 18% of National's stock to Peter Grace.

These transactions cut Baker's holding to approximately

12%, but Baker, with Grace and other large stockholders such as Lou Bower, could still outvote Trippe with his 30%. Again it appeared to be a stalemate. Grace, Trippe, and Baker waited with all the patience of professional poker players until the hearing actually was under way before the Civil Aeronautics Board in the dismemberment case. Then Trippe, who had been forced into the game, apparently decided that he held the weakest hand.

One afternoon, after the Docket 3500 proceedings had started, Grace, Baker, and Trippe met in a Washington hotel suite. The meeting was a private one, but it has been reported that Baker told Trippe that a canvass of the majority of the stockholders in National revealed that a merger with Panagra had been approved as the best solution to National's problems. There was, however, one alternative. If Pan American would support the proposed three-way interchange between New York and South America by National, Pan Am, and Panagra, then it was quite possible that the CAB would support a motion for continuance of the hearings because of the unanticipated development.

Trippe was in a quandary. By controlling 50% of Panagra he could effectively block the proposed merger between Panagra and National. But by so doing, he ran the risk of being labeled an obstructionist by the CAB, and this might reflect negatively upon Pan Am in the future. On the other hand, by agreeing to the interchange, he could still block Panagra from applying for the route from Balboa, Canal Zone, to Miami, the Pan American portion of the interchange. Conversely, if the proposal did remove the threat of National's dismemberment, there would be nothing to prevent National from applying for a certificate to fly between Miami and Balboa.

No one other than the principals know in detail what was discussed during this meeting. It is known that it lasted until four the following morning, and by that time a memorandum of understanding that agreed to the establishment of an inter-change, subject to the Board's approval, was signed by Baker, Grace, and Trippe.

John Cross, representing National, was a party to some of the discussions among the three airline heads.

"This actually took place, and I remember it was an all-night sesssion," Cross recalls. "We negotiated an equipment interchange and a stock sale. [When it was over] I took a shower and then went directly to the hearings. I never did get to go home and never did get to go to bed. Wilbur Morrison [a Pan American vice president] had been on the stand the day before. He had not been advised of the negotiations, because no one knew whether or not they were going to result in an agreement. He was testifying against National, and the next morning he walked in and found out that he was a partner of theirs. This completely changed the complexion of the hearing and of his testimony. We advised Francis Brown, the examiner in charge of the hearing, of what had happened, made a statement to this effect on the record, and as a result the hearing was adjourned."

Baker had won the necessary time to save the airline. He also had money from the sale of stock to Grace. And for a man who was customarily blunt-spoken and often abrasive, he had displayed a remarkable skill in the corporate political arena.

During the long adjournment, Trippe quietly began buy-ing up National stock in the open market, obviously hoping to gain control of the airline the same way Howard Hughes gained control of Trans World Airlines.

The 174,000 shares that had been sold to Grace were the last unissued stock of the then capitalization of one million shares. To meet the proposed stock commitments to Pan Am in connection with the three-way interchange agreement, Na-tional's stockholders approved a further issue of six hundred thousand shares.

As the months dragged on, lawyers for the three carriers

dickered over the rate to be paid on the leased planes under the pact and could reach no agreement. In December of 1950 Baker apparently learned for the first time that Trippe was buying up National stock on the open market. Baker reacted by tearing up the option agreement that had been signed in the Washington hotel room. The agreement, he contended, limited Trippe's stock ownership in National to 30%. Thus, by buying additional stock, Trippe had breached the contract. At the same time, he announced that National still considered the agreement for the interchange to be valid.

Trippe fought back angrily. He said that the agreements were interdependent and that Baker, by repudiating the stock option, had also repudiated the interchange agreement. As could be expected, with Juan Trippe going one way, Peter Grace went the other and sided with National. The Civil Aeronautics Board also agreed with National and Panagra. Pan Am countered by pointing out that it was half owner of Panagra and that it was Pan Am that ran the Balboa–Miami segment of the proposed interchange. Because of this, Pan Am's agreement was necessary to the formation of any interchange. The CAB finally settled this by deciding to start all over again with new hearings on the case. Baker then applied for a route extension from Miami to Balboa. This is how the proposal rested for nearly five years, until an agreement was reached and created the operation of the three-way interchange. National never withdrew its application for service to Balboa.

There is another factor to Docket 3500. It is a reasonable assumption that the proceedings were triggered by political pressure, first from labor and then from other carriers who wanted a portion of the booty. Still, the CAB could not ethically initiate proceedings to kill a carrier merely because of a dispute with labor or because other carriers wanted the routes. In 1948, when Docket 3500 was initiated, National was in a precarious financial position, and many persons in the airline industry, including John Cross, believe that the CAB genuinely was concerned over National's ability to survive as an independent carrier. During 1948 there was a minor recession, and National was suffering heavy financial losses. During this era, trunk carriers were eligible for federal subsidy, and the losses were being balanced by the federal treasury. Cross also is not convinced that National would have been dismembered had there been no ploy by Baker with Juan Trippe.

"The unions were fighting National with everything they had. That was one angle of it," he says. "And of course there were other carriers that were trying to obtain our routes. But we tried Docket 3500 on the theory that if we could keep it going long enough, the Board would never dismember National. We knew we were in a low period in the financial history of the company, but we just knew the patient would get well if we could keep the case going long enough."

Baker, however, always retained a dour attitude toward the unions. Several years later, when a contract for ramp agents and other allied personnel was in the process of negotiation, Baker met a youthful ramp agent in Newark named Paul Donnini.

"Will you loan me five dollars?" Baker asked Donnini.

"Yes, sir." Donnini reached for his wallet.

Baker waved him away. "And you guys are supposed to be hurting for dough," he said.

The airline did become healthy, and its recovery was rapid. There were two basic contributing factors. One was the purchase by Grace of the 174,000 shares of stock for $957,-000. The other was an intensive drive to turn Miami into an all-year resort, which would stimulate the load factors during the summer months. Although in his memoirs Rickenbacker takes credit for this promotion, the credit rightfully belongs to Baker. In co-operation with many of the hotels on Miami Beach, he worked out an assortment of package vacations, in

which both air fares and hotel rates were slashed to the minimum. Baker became an apostle of cut rates and low fares.
He borrowed the night coach-fare idea from Capitol Airlines
and introduced it on the East Coast, then went one step
further and proposed similar "day coach" fares. Eastern
objected strenuously to the "day coach" proposal and carried
its fight to the Civil Aeronautics Board. There is an amusing
incident in connection with this fight.

In 1940, when Baker went to Los Angeles to negotiate
the purchase of National's first Lodestars, he was introduced
to the quite beautiful motion picture actress Irma Wilson, and
approximately a year later, after many trips by Baker to Los
Angeles, the two were married. Irma Baker, because of her
beauty and charm, very shortly became as well-known in airline circles as Ted.

During the hearing, Baker was called to the stand to be in-
terrogated by an Eastern Airlines attorney who had been
introduced to Irma at a Washington reception the night before.
"What percentage of stock do you control in National?" the
attorney asked.

"About 17%."

The lawyer riffled through some papers. "This includes
stock that your wife owns?"

Baker agreed that it did.

"What makes you think your wife will vote her stock the
same way you do?" the attorney pressed.

Baker leaned back in his chair. "I will tell you," he replied. "Every night, after we go upstairs and are getting ready
for bed, my wife comes over and puts her lily-white arms
around my neck and whispers in my ear. And what she tells
me is this. She says, 'Ted, you vote my stock any way you
want to.'"

The usually staid CAB hearings convulsed in laughter.

The next day, day-coach fares were approved by the CAB.

In 1948, the year of the prolonged strike, National's net
loss was $1,946,000. The following year, after the strike settle-

ment, the airline showed a net profit of $39,000, and in 1950 the carrier showed a net profit of $558,000.

In March of 1951 the CAB quietly dismissed Docket 3500. In a short announcement that accompanied the dismissal notice, the CAB said: "The position of National in the air transportation industry has changed substantially since the institution of this proceeding, at which time National was in a precarious financial position.

"The record establishes that National has held its own since relieved of the causes leading to its bad performance in 1948, and an analysis of National's overall performance between the years of 1944 and 1950, exclusive of 1948, leads to the conclusion that National should continue to do as well as any other carrier in its class. As a matter of fact, National's most recent figures tend to show that continued performance for future periods may well result in its becoming self-sufficient."

Only one other minor matter remained for Baker to clean up—the 174,000 shares of National that were owned by Grace. Shortly after the dismissal of Docket 3500, Baker and Grace got together, and the latter agreed, after a period of negotiation, to sell the shares back to Baker, but at a price that would net Grace $1½-million profit.

This transaction did not go off as smoothly as Baker wished. One member of National's board, William K. Jacobs, Jr., had been harshly critical of Baker from the moment the pilots went out on strike. At first Baker privately referred to Jacobs as the ALPA representative on the board. Later, he referred to him as "Trippe's man."

When Baker bought back Grace's holdings in National at a $1½-million loss, Jacobs charged openly that the transaction was illegal, because the purchase had been consummated without the approval of National's board of directors.

"Not so," Baker replied blandly and added that he had contacted all the directors by telephone and received their approval—all except Jacobs, that was, who for some reason or another had not been within reach.

Jacobs had been on National's board since 1942, but in 1951 he was dropped from management's slate. A small insurgent group of stockholders had rallied behind him in support of his proxy fight to oust Baker. The fight centered around three management proposals. The most important, from both Jacobs' and Baker's points of view, was Baker's plan to eliminate from the incorporation certificate and bylaws a provision for cumulative voting for directors. This was a system that gave each stockholder as many votes as there were directors to be elected, allowing him to use them all on one candidate or distribute them according to his choice. Under this system, it was almost impossible to remove Jacobs from the board. Understandably, Jacobs wished to retain cumulative voting.

The second item objected to by Jacobs was a Baker proposal to substitute a simple majority vote for the required two-thirds vote by either the directors or stockholders. Jacobs also was demanding that the 588,465 shares of stock reserved for the three-way interchange agreement be made available for general corporate purposes.

Both factions freely aired their views in the press. Jacobs claimed Baker was trying to take advantage of the stockholders to make himself absolute dictator of the carrier. Baker called Jacobs a troublemaker and said he wanted cumulative voting abolished to make sure that "minority groups with special interests" did not get on the board in the future. The other changes were simply "routine."

The issue came to a head in the 1951 annual meeting of the airline, which was held in National Airlines' general offices. Baker hired more armed guards to maintain "security" than were present at the last Democratic convention and announced that the press would be barred. One Miami reporter promptly bought one share of National stock and went in as a National stockholder.

The Jacobs faction arrived with a large contingent of armed men from the Burns Detective Agency.

In the airline's minutes of the meeting is the following dialogue.

"Where are your guns?"

"We parked them at the door."

Jacobs did not have the support on which he had been counting. The majority of the stockholders backed Baker in his drive to eliminate cumulative voting and thus, in effect, win stockholder approval of the repurchase of the Grace stock, and at the same time they enabled Baker to have Jacobs removed from the board of directors.

Almost three years, to the day, after the initiation of Docket 3500, Baker was firmly in charge of his airline again.

CHAPTER NINE

In the latter part of September of 1961, about two weeks after Maytag's second visit to Miami, Baker called John Cross in Washington. "When you get a chance, I would like you to get in touch with Bob Six and see if he still is interested in a merger," Baker said.

A couple of years earlier, the CAB had been in the middle of a Trans-Pacific Route case, "the first one," which was shelved later at the instigation of President Eisenhower. One of the applicants in this case had been Continental Airlines. Continental's president, Robert Six, had called John Cross, asking the attorney to represent him.

Here there was no conflict of interest. Continental's route did not connect anywhere with National at this time, and National was not an applicant in the Trans-Pacific Route case. Both carriers, however, were applicants in the Southern Transcontinental Route case, and from an ethical point of view, John Cross felt he should get a reaction from Baker before accepting the Continental offer.

"Somewhat to my surprise, Ted was not really opposed to it," Cross recalls. "He said, 'Well, let me think about it.'"

A few days later, Cross called Baker again. Baker had no objections, and he commented that he always had felt that Bob Six was a very good friend. Some months later, Baker was in Washington and hinted that he would like to see Six and possibly discuss the pros and cons of a merger. A meeting was arranged, and both men were enthused over such a possibility. Continental had a large portion of the West; National a similar portion of the East. Because both carriers were applicants in the Southern Transcontinental Route case, however, both Six and Baker deemed it prudent to withhold any merger plans until after the case was decided. They could not afford to come in with a merger proposal during the pendency of the case, because it could have defeated both their applications.

Six was confident that Continental would be extended to the East, at least as far as Houston, once the case was decided. Baker was less confident of any route expansion because of his long drought. His market on the East Coast had fallen off because of the increased competiton from Northeast; the future appeared dim in Cuba. If he got nothing in the Southern Transcontinental Route case, he could link up with Continental in Houston.

"I rather think this is what Ted had in mind when he told me to go ahead and represent Bob," Cross says. "There were no details or any agreement worked out. Somewhere along the line, both of them said to me that maybe National and Continental should make a deal."

It was a little more than three months after service was suspended to Cuba that the Civil Aeronautics Board announced its decisions in the Southern Transcontinental Route case. National was one of the prime beneficiaries, when it was extended west to Las Vegas, Los Angeles, San Francisco, and San Diego. As Bob Six had anticipated, Continental was extended to the East as far as Houston, but instead of the expected linkup with National, the two carriers now found themselves competing on the Los Angeles–Houston route segment.

Service on the Southern Transcontinental Route was inaugurated, as mentioned in Chapter One, on June 11, 1961. Then, in the latter part of September, more than three months after he had started negotiations with Maytag, Baker told Cross to reopen the merger discussions with Continental.

Six was indeed interested in merger. He flew to Miami, and the fundamentals of the agreement were reached quickly. The surviving carrier was to be National. Six would be president and Baker would become chairman of the board. The consolidation would be effected by an exchange of stock.

It took several weeks for the lawyers to transfer the basic agreement into legal parlance, and it was not until December 12 that the proposal was filed with the Civil Aeronautics Board. During these weeks, Maytag spoke with Baker twice, but the National president did not bother to mention that he was working on a merger with Continental. Announcement of the proposed merger was made, on the day of the filing, simultaneously by Baker in Miami and Six from Continental's headquarters in Denver, Colorado.

In an office building nearby, in another part of Stapleton Field, in Denver, the news of the merger announcement was greeted with "something closely resembling consternation."

"Then we rationalized that it was rather typical of Mr. Baker to do something like this," Ray Woody says. "No one ever has disputed the fact that his behavior was consistently erratic."

Bud Maytag's immediate reaction, when he read of the proposed merger in the Denver *Post,* was to pick up the telephone and call Baker in Miami.

"Oh, come on now," Baker said in the bland manner he could adopt when needed. "This hasn't got anything to do with our deal."

"What do you mean, it doesn't make any difference? You're talking about a whole new airline."

"Aw, forget it. You buy my part and walk in just where I am."

Maytag slowly shook his head as he hung up. He put his feet on his desk, tipped back in his chair, and clasped his hands behind his head. Even the most elementary agreement on such a merger as that proposed between Continental and National would require a considerable amount of work from the legal departments of both airlines. Prior to this, there necessarily would have been meetings to establish the nucleus of an agreement between the two principals, Bob Six and Ted Baker. Thus, Baker had been dealing with Six at the same time he had been dealing with one Bud Maytag. This being the case, Baker could be dealing with several other persons also. Six, however, was in a vulnerable spot, because he was now out in the open and because it would take many, many months to process a merger of two trunk carriers through the Civil Aeronautics Board. In addition, there was no communality between the two carriers. They competed on only one route, between Los Angeles and Houston. On almost every other major route, Continental was bracketed by one or two of the big three. There was no similarity in equipment, other than obsolete DC-6s, which both carriers were using on local runs. Continental flew Boeing 707s and Viscounts. National flew DC-8s and Electras. Both Bob Six and Ted Baker were mercurial men, each used to completely dominating his own airline. It was difficult to see how one would defer to the other in the operation of the proposed carrier. Maytag smiled. The whole thing could be a ploy upon Baker's part to build up pressure on one Bud Maytag and force him to move a little quicker. If this was the case, Baker really wanted to get out, and he might give a little on the thirty-five-dollar-a-share price. On the other hand, Baker really might be serious in going the merger route.

Maytag shrugged. There was nothing he could do about it until he sold Frontier.

In Miami, the proposed merger became a point of discussion for some key executives in the Storer Broadcasting Corporation. "It looks like the object of our attentions got married before we got around to wooing her," one executive said.

"It does indeed," another agreed.

Preliminary plans for the Storer Broadcasting Company to

THE ANATOMY OF AN AIRLINE

approach Baker with an offer to buy out his holdings were
shelved.

With Docket 3500 safely behind him, Baker once again
became preoccupied with expansion of the airline. In view
of the CAB's announced policy at the time of not approving
any new route applications, this left Baker only the alternatives
of acquisition and merger. The merger candidates were shy,
because all the executives in the airline industry were well
aware of what had happened to the "merger" with Panagra.
Baker always had been merger-conscious.

Baker approached Northwest Airlines, and a series of talks
over a proposed merger were held in Minneapolis and Miami,
but here, again, no agreement was reached. He made over-
tures to Northeast, but at this time Delta was negotiating with
the New England carrier, and he was rebuffed. He next turned
to Colonial Airlines.

Colonial was a comparatively small carrier, controlled by a
Sigmund Janus. Its route structure extended from Bermuda
to New York and Washington, and through several Pennsylvania and upstate New York cities into Ottawa and Montreal, Canada. An agreement was drawn up under which
National would absorb Colonial in return for the distribution
of 450,151 shares of National stock to Colonial's stockholders,
or seven shares of National stock in exchange for eight shares
of Colonial. There appeared to be no question as to the agreement being approved by the stockholders of both companies
and the Civil Aeronautics Board.

At the end of World War II, Baker had attempted to take
over Caribbean Atlantic Airlines, a San Juan, Puerto Rico-
based carrier better known as Caribair. Baker's tactics did not
precisely follow the CAB book of rules and regulations.

There were two attorneys in Miami, named Anderson and
Scott, both of whom represented National. They formed a new
company known as the ANSCO Charter Service, which
chartered planes exclusively from National. In return for this

consideration, National sold tickets on the charter flights that ran back and forth between San Juan and Miami.

Caribair has routes down the Caribbean archipelago, and because of the quick success of the ANSCO Charter Service, Baker decided to buy out Caribair. By so doing, he thought he could apply to the CAB successfully for permission to link up his two routes by getting authorization to fly between San Juan and Miami. Until such permission was granted, he could continue with his ANSCO charters and possibly extend them as far south as Trinidad.

At that time Caribair was controlled by Dennis Powelson, and at a meeting in Miami's Columbus Hotel, Powelson and Baker signed the necessary papers that transferred Powelson's stock to Baker. Acting on the presumption that the take-over was an accomplished fact, Baker sent key personnel from National to San Juan and allowed National airplanes to go into service on Caribair's routes without even the pretense of a charter.

The CAB, however, adopted a most dim view of Baker's presumption and issued a cease and desist order. Reluctantly Baker called back his personnel. One man, L. A. (Luke) Lockhart, ignored the call and today is treasurer of Caribair in San Juan. An angry Powelson refused to let one of the Lodestars return to Miami.

It was Powelson's contention that Baker had made a deal and had to go through with it no matter what the CAB ruled.

"I can't; it's illegal," Baker protested at a stormy meeting in his office at National in Miami.

"It wasn't illegal when we made it," Powelson retorted. "If you have trouble with the CAB, that's your problem. You've bought my stock and you're going to pay for it."

Baker did not pay for it. Powelson sued him, for some unknown reason in the State of Mississippi. The case dragged on for years and finally was dismissed when Powelson was killed in a plane accident in South America. The Lodestar was recovered long before the suit was abandoned. Baker had a federal marshal impound it on its first flight to the Virgin Islands, when it was put into use by Caribair. Also dropped were the ANSCO charters.

In its cease and desist order, the CAB was blunt:

"The legislative authorization to acquire control of another carrier is expressly contingent upon obtaining approval of the Board," the CAB said, "and if approval of acquisition of control were to be accomplished widely in the same manner sought to be employed here, our efforts toward the proper administration of the Act from the long-range point of view would be hampered, with attendant substantial menace to the public."

Yet, a few years later, Eastern torpedoed National in its bid to buy Colonial in much the same manner that Baker had sought to take over control of Caribair. It is unknown when Baker first became aware that all was not well with the Colonial deal, but it is known that he learned that large stockholders in Eastern were buying up large blocks of stock in Colonial.

One of the stockholders in Colonial was a rich New York industrialist who owned a "fishing camp" in central Florida. Baker found out that the New Yorker was in his hideaway and, unannounced, went to see him. The industrialist was sitting on the pier, fishing. Baker apologized for the interruption, then hinted that he had come to see if the man's stock in Colonial was for sale.

"Well, it was," came the reply, "but I sold it two days ago to one of the fellows from Eastern Airlines."

Baker had become aware of the situation much too late to catch up with his old rival, Eddie Rickenbacker. When he checked with Colonial upon his return to Miami, he was told only that Eastern also was bidding on the Colonial acquisition.

In a brief filed later with the CAB, National said: "National was notified by Colonial's vice president in a last-minute telephone call that several changes were made by Eastern in the bidding form. National was asked if they would like to suggest any changes. Accordingly, National, through its assistant vice president, suggested one single change in the bidding form—namely, to limit the bidding to common stock. This single request was denied on the telephone by Colonial's vice president. In fact, it is now obvious from the record that National's request was not even relayed to the president or its board of directors, whereas Eastern and Colonial had a meeting among Rickenbacker and several others about the Eastern changes in bidding forms requested earlier. Furthermore, the meeting was held in the offices of Rickenbacker and on Eastern property, and the changes in the bidding form requested by Eastern were made and reported in the corporate minutes of Colonial Airlines."

The board of directors of Colonial Airlines approved of the proposed merger with National and recommended approval of the transaction to their stockholders. When the proposal was put to the stockholders, however, it was rejected by a majority. Baker was furious.

"He not only was mad that he had lost Colonial," a former National officer says, "but what irritated him more was the fact that he had been taken by Rickenbacker."

Baker was not the only one upset over the transaction. There are some who say Baker "raised so much hell, that everyone got into the act." The proposed merger did draw the attention of "everyone," including Board counsel, the Department of Justice, and even the President of the United States. The transaction required the approval of the President because it involved routes outside the United States, and Eisenhower would not sign it. The Civil Aeronautics Board then set up an investigation of the transaction known as Docket 5666. Baker, understandably, was elated.

The percentage paid by Eastern for Colonial over the book value was 344.51%, which was a new high for the industry. The examiner conducting the Docket 5666 investigation found that "about 110,000 shares of Colonial stock or approximately 21 percent of all the capital stock of the carrier were acquired by two of Eastern's directors and persons and firms in the immediate orbit of Eastern's influence." No specific recapitulation of the stockholders was included in the 110,000 figure used by the examiner in his report made in Docket 5666, so a definite listing of such stockholders is now impossible.

With the investigators from the Civil Aeronautics Board breathing down their necks, some of the stockholders within the Eastern orbit bailed out—sold their stock. At the conclusion of the investigation, Baker had good reason to feel elated and confident that the National-Colonial merger would go through.

The Bureau of Public Affairs counsel was extraordinarily rough on Eastern. "A more brazen and willful demonstration of the employment of stock control power to compel a corporation management to accept the offer of a designated bidder, in this case, Eastern, by pointedly demanding a meeting for the sole purpose of considering only that one offer, is difficult to imagine.

"Its coercive effect upon the badgered and bewildered Colonial management still reeling from the stockholder rejection of the recommendation of approval of a merger with National needs no amplification."

After the Docket 5666 investigation, the CAB apparently felt the need to issue an explanation for its approval of the Eastern-Colonial merger.

In its Order, Serial Number E-8446, the Board said: ". . . only the President's approval was required to actuate the merger and thus eliminate Colonial as a subsidy carrier costing the government approximately $850,000 a year to support. On the other hand, had we disapproved the Eastern-Colonial agreement, we would have had no assurance at that time that Colonial would enter into an agreement with National or any other airline, and the subsidy payments to Colonial would continue during future negotiations and perhaps for an indefinite period.

"In this posture, we felt that the savings to the government and other advantages of the Eastern-Colonial merger were considerations for approval of such weight to overbalance the public interest in preserving the integrity of Section 408 of the Act. Subsequently, at the direction of the President, we found the Eastern-Colonial acquisition agreement should be disapproved because of the Eastern violation of Section 408. The issue now before us is: What action, if any, should the Board now take with regard to possible integration involving Colonial?

"We have determined that it is in the public interest to proceed at this time to the merits of the investigation of a possible National-Colonial merger. We find on the basis of existing records that a National-Colonial integration would be consistent with the public interest. Such a finding is amply supported by the record."

The day after the order came out, a Friday, there was no "bloodletting ritual" in the executive dining room in National's general office. Baker was extraordinarily mellow. "We've got Bermuda and Canada in the bag," he confided to John Morris.

Baker's optimism was very premature. Almost immediately, he discovered that he had incurred the resentment of almost all the stockholders in Colonial and that this resentment now was being reflected by Colonial's management and board. The crux of the matter was that Baker simply did not have enough money, nor could he raise enough money, to outbid Rickenbacker for Colonial. By December 31, 1954, more than two years after Baker had originally started the negotiations with Colonial, Eastern still was offering to pay $9,670,145 for Colonial's assets although Colonial's book value on the same date was, according to the examiner, $2,175,442.

Baker was stalling the proceedings by arguing that Colonial still was illegally controlled by Eastern, and the briefs that were filed in support of his contention were vitriolic. One of them started, "Eastern is a lawbreaker. . . . a law violator should not be rewarded with the fruits of such violation." Baker's strategy was based on the assumption that he could have Eastern removed permanently from the case and then take over Colonial for a figure that more closely matched Colonial's book value. This was hitting the Colonial stockholders in the pocketbooks, and they did not like it. They no longer wanted National. They wanted Eastern.

The Colonial management finally came up with a solution. The corporate minutes of a meeting on May 14, 1954, explain the plan. "The Board was informed that a stockholder holding a substantial amount of Colonial stock has suggested that all of the holders of Colonial stock who were alleged to have been under the influence of Eastern, should take whatever action is necessary to remove any shadow of a doubt. He further suggested that the Corporation should consider assuming the responsibility to present these matters to these particular stockholders with a view toward establishing an arrangement which would place the voting power in the hands of an independent person with authority to vote the stock in favor of the highest offer received from either National or Eastern."

The proposed voting trust was adopted at a Colonial meeting August 12, and the first Baker heard about it was when Colonial made it public in a petition filed with the CAB.

By now, however, it did not make any difference whether the large block of stock within "Eastern's orbit of influence" was voted or not. What it did mean was that Baker could either top Rickenbacker's offer or get out. There were some more hearings held in the matter, but the Civil Aeronautics Board accepted the voting trust solution. Baker could not meet the price.

Under the voting trust agreement, the matter once again was put to the Colonial stockholders to choose between the $9½-million offer by Eastern and the $2½-million offer by National.

Again the Eastern-Colonial merger was approved by the Civil Aeronautics Board, and this time President Eisenhower signed it when it came across his desk.

In his lengthy memoirs, *"Rickenbacker,"* (Prentice-Hall, 1967), Rickenbacker devotes only a brief paragraph to the lengthy Colonial imbroglio. "We reached Canada and Bermuda by purchasing Colonial Airlines, which had routes from New York to Montreal and Ottawa in Canada, and Bermuda," he says. "Later we gave Colonial's local service in New York and New England to Mohawk Airlines."

This has an ironic twist. Ostensibly, the whole purpose of the Colonial merger was to remove that carrier from subsidy. Yet, when most of its routes were given to Mohawk, the system promptly went back on subsidy.

Baker next turned his attention to Northeast Airlines. Northeast was operating in the New England area with a very heavy subsidy. Its southern terminal point was New York, and it was fighting for an entry into the East Coast market from New York as far south as Miami. It offered the usual contention of most regional carriers that such a long-haul extension would reduce its subsidy, to the benefit of the taxpayers. Northeast was not the only carrier seeking to enter this market. Other applicants were Delta, Pan American, and Chicago & Southern, and probably for the first time, Eastern and National found themselves allied in trying to keep all the other applicants out of the market. At the same time, National applied for service to Providence and Boston.

Baker then announced that he was willing to buy Northeast Airlines outright and operate it without subsidy. Eastern thought this was an excellent idea.

"Since Eastern entered into a contract to acquire Colonial Airlines, Eastern has taken the position that the logical solution for Northeast's problems is merger or other consolidation with National Airlines," William A. Morrisette, Jr., Eastern's vice president of traffic and sales, announced.

It apparently was a political ploy on the part of Baker and Rickenbacker, but it failed. Donald R. Larrabee, writing in the *Washington Forecast,* said Baker's offer was an attempt to put Northeast on the defensive. "But Examiner (Thomas

L.) Wrenn seems to have sidetracked questioning on this proposal by ruling out any discussion of prices or conditions. The CAB ruled that such questions were beyond the scope of the hearings before it [sic] started."

It cannot be determined now whether or not Baker was serious in his bid to buy Northeast. Some say he was and some say he was not. If he was serious, then his offer was not a wise one, as he would be only picking up some antiquated DC-3s and DC-6s of Northeast along with some routes throughout New England that still are unprofitable today. The question before the CAB was whether or not to put a third carrier on the New York–Miami run. Thus, if National had acquired Northeast, it would be competing with Eastern and another carrier on the New York–Miami run. It is always preferable to compete with a weak carrier than a strong one. Thus, Baker's motivations are a mystery. The offer made neither political nor financial sense.

Several years later, Eastern and National jointly offered to buy the nearly bankrupt Northeast, which was given the route, and turn over the New England route segments to another regional carrier, but this offer was rejected.

During his testimony before the CAB, Baker digressed to announce that National Airlines had placed orders for six Douglas DC-8 jetliners and that it had received definite delivery dates for these aircraft. Actually Baker had only ordered three DC-8s, with options for three more. It made National the first domestic carrier to announce definite orders for an American-built jet airliner. The purchase price was $4,600,000 for each plane, which is just about half of what a standard DC-8 costs today. There is an interesting story as to why the price was so low and why Douglas won out over Boeing in selling National jet equipment.

Baker preferred the medium-range Boeing 720 jet, and although he had made his choice, he characteristically continued to haggle with the representatives of both companies, who were in Miami.

One evening, after more than a month of haggling, Ben Guaneri, who headed the Boeing sales team, received a telephone call from his general office in Seattle. The early delivery positions on the 720 were gone. They had been sold to a Central American carrier. The following morning, Guaneri reluctantly broke the news to Baker.

"Has it been announced?" Baker asked.

Guaneri shook his head.

"Then you just stick around for a few more days and keep this to yourself," Baker told Guaneri, and the Boeing sales executive agreed.

Baker next summoned the Douglas sales team and made them an offer. If Douglas would sell him three DC-8s for the same price as the Boeing 720, they could make a deal, but he had to have an answer right away.

Baker got the answer right away. Douglas, who was trailing Boeing in advance sales of jets, was just delighted to get its jets into National. It agreed to meet Baker's price.

Today, although the preponderance of National's fleet is Boeing equipment, it has fifteen DC-8s, representing a total sales value to Douglas in excess of one hundred million dollars.

Ironically, shortly after Baker made his deal with Douglas, Guaneri, who still was in Miami, received another telephone call from Seattle. The sale to the Central American carrier had fallen apart. The early delivery positions once again were open.

Northeast was granted a temporary certificate in 1956 to fly between New York and Miami. The route award was made permanent in 1965, after Northeast had completed almost a decade of financial disaster before being purchased by the Storer Broadcasting Company.

Shortly after Northeast was placed in the New York–Miami run, National was granted a temporary certificate that extended it westward to Houston.

The customary inaugural flight was launched, and among

the "very important persons" on board was a Miami congressman. Several civic leaders were waiting inside the terminal building to greet it. The congressman, who had the politician's talent to attract attention, rushed to be first out the door of the National plane. When he reached the bottom of the steps, an Eastern Constellation started an engine with a roar and deposited a layer of dust, oil, and smoke from its propwash over the startled congressman.

Baker immediately ordered one of his aides to drive the politician on ahead to his hotel in order that he might bathe and get into clean clothes, then turned back to his functions with the welcoming committee.

A quarter hour later, Baker noticed the congressman, his face still smeared with dust and grime, standing as unobtrusively as possible near the door. Baker went over to him, apologized again, then pointed out that it was an Eastern plane that had caused the congressman's discomfort.

The politician nodded. "But it wasn't Eastern who left all my luggage behind in Miami," he replied.

A few months later, National also was extended north from New York to Providence, Rhode Island, and Boston, Massachusetts.

Another significant event occurred in 1956, but it attracted no attention in the National hierarchy at the time. It was the year that a bearded young revolutionary made his first eventually successful bid for power in Cuba and whose ultimate seizure of the government was to mark the end of an era for the airline.

CHAPTER TEN

The word was being spread quietly around the country that Frontier Airlines was for sale, and eventually it reached the ears of a gentleman named Marvin Tavel, a very competent promoter, who came to Denver to see Maytag. Tavel's proposition was succinct. For a fee of one hundred thousand dollars, he could find someone to buy Frontier, and he would handle the situation in a discreet manner. Maytag agreed to the proposition. It is quite possible that Tavel had his prospect pegged before he approached Maytag, because it was very shortly after his departure that Maytag received a telephone call from New York.

No one now remembers the date, or which day of the week it was when the overture was made, but everyone does recall that it was in January and that the temperature in Denver was 34° below zero. At the same time, there were several National personnel of management level in the city to iron out problems that always arise in a merger between two corporations such as National and Continental. Some of these people were native Floridians, who were amazed that one could survive in such temperatures.

The man who was interested in buying Frontier was Richard C. Pistell, a wealthy New York executive who, among other things, was chairman of the board of the Goldfield Corporation. "Marvin Tavel tells me you have an airline for sale," Pistell said.

"Yes, it's for sale," Bud Maytag replied. "I'm asking five dollars a share and cash, and no hanky-panky deals."

"I'm interested," Pistell said. "When can we get together?"

"It's probably a little warmer back in New York than it is here."

When Pistell heard how cold it was in Denver, he thought New York was an excellent place to meet and suggested lunch on the following day.

Pistell is a shrewd businessman, Maytag recalls, and the first meeting between them was more or less a preliminary skirmish. "He was trying to find out how firm I was on my price. I was firm. I had to be if I was going to get enough money to buy Baker's interest in National. I explained to him that I wanted five dollars a share, and that, if he could come up with the cash, we had a deal. We didn't get very close to an agreement, so I went back to Denver."

There were several other calls. Pistell wanted to negotiate, but Maytag would not budge. It was not that he objected to negotiation. He knew that he needed the five-dollars-a-share price if he was to be successful in acquiring control of National.

Several days after the New York meeting, Maytag received a call from John Love, his attorney. "I have just talked to Mr. Pistell in New York, and he says he wants to buy your airline," Love said.

"What did you tell him?"

Love laughed. "I just told him that if he showed up with the money and walked in on you, I could see no reason why he wouldn't have a deal."

Pistell took Love's advice seriously. Two days after he talked to the attorney he was in Denver.

"He called up, said he was in town, and that he would like to see me. Of course I agreed, and about an hour later he showed up at the office. 'Here's a check for cash at the price we agreed on of five dollars a share,' he said. 'You can take the check and let the lawyers work out the details and I'll get out of your hair.' I couldn't believe it. I just said okay and took the check."

Just before Pistell left, Maytag told Pistell that he was taking four men with him.

"Which four?"

"Ray Woody, executive vice president, Ed Dolansky, vice president of finance, Dan Brock, vice president of sales, and Bill Nelson, vice president of legal."

"That's the whole airline," Pistell protested.

"You can find somebody easily," Maytag replied.

For a moment Pistell hesitated; then he shrugged, shook hands, and departed.

The lawyers, under pressure from both Maytag and Pistell, only took about ten days to draw up the sales contract. When the transaction was finished, Maytag called Baker in Miami. "I've sold Frontier," he said. "Now I'd like to come down and talk to you again about buying National."

Baker paused noticeably before he replied. "Any time you say."

"I'm going to bring John Love with me. He's my attorney."

"I'll ask John Cross to come down from Washington." Again Baker paused, then added, "I'll have a suite at the International Hotel. That will save you the trouble of coming over to the office."

Maytag smiled to himself. Baker was becoming very solicitous, he thought, or possibly there were as many Continental people swarming around National's general offices as there were National people in Continental's general office.

Robert Six was in Miami at the time of Maytag's telephone call, and a short time later, Baker broke the news to Six that the merger was off. Six was furious, "although he shook hands with Baker like a gentleman," Cross recalls.

A short statement was written for the press announcing that the merger had been called off by mutual agreement of both Six and Baker, and both men also agreed to release it simultaneously the following morning.

About a half hour after Six left the building, Baker noticed Jane Wood in the foyer of the executive offices. She worked for Hank Meyer & Associates, a public-relations agency retained by the airline. Baker called her into the office and gave her the statement.

She noticed the date on the statement. "You want this to go tomorrow morning?" she asked.

Baker shook his head. "Put it out right now," he said.

People close to Six say that he believes Maytag got the idea to buy control of National after the announcement of the proposed merger had been made. He still finds the experience distasteful and will not discuss it. Friends of Baker, such as Lew Dymond, contend that Baker never was convinced that Maytag was going to buy control of National and that the merger negotiation with the temperamental Six "was just something cooking on the back burner."

John Cross indicates that Baker knew his time was running out and that he was anxious to put together some kind of deal. "Ted knew he had a serious heart condition, and Ted knew several years before that he had to have a little money in the bank. The Maytag offer was a cash offer. The Continental offer was simply an exchange of stock. In the long run, it might have been a better deal to take the Continental offer, but it didn't relieve Ted's cash problems so far as the estate was concerned."

Another thought that has been voiced is that Baker was trying to apply pressure on Maytag to make him move more quickly and that he had no intention of going through with the Continental merger. Supporting this theory is the fact that Six surely had no indication that Baker had been negotiating with Maytag when he reopened the merger discussions with Six.

The date for the next meeting between Baker and Maytag was scheduled for approximately a week after the telephone call. That evening, as Maytag was driving to his home, he heard an announcement on a newscast over the car radio.

"In a joint announcement, National Airlines and Continental Airlines reported today that they had been unable to finalize merger plans announced last month."

Maytag smiled inwardly and wondered how much Baker really wanted for his stock.

The carriers are very aware of what they term their "interline" relationships, because much of the business of one carrier comes from the feed of another. For example, LAN, the Chilean national airline, goes into South America from Miami and New York only, yet it maintains a large sales office on the West Coast. Their personnel in this office sell seats into South America from Miami, and the way they connect their passengers to their flights is to fly them from California to Miami on National. These "tie-ins" work over most of the world's route structures.

During the latter part of World War II, Baker, by chance, was in Key West and discovered that the president of Aerovías Q., Colonel Manuel Quevada, also was in Key West, which was the North American terminal point for the Cuban airline.

Quevada was a close friend of Cuban President Fulgencio Batista. There is a story told, which may be apocryphal, that when Batista seized control of the Cuban Government for the first time, in August of 1933, he sent Quevada a telegram saying that effective immediately "you are promoted to the rank of captain. Acknowledge."

Quevada wired back: "Your telegram arrived too late. I had already promoted myself to colonel." And colonel he remained.

In 1944, when Batista was defeated in the elections by Dr. Ramón Grau San Martín, Quevada kept his rank in the Cuban Air Force and also his position as owner and president of Aerovías Q. Quevada's carrier operated domestically within Cuba and also had one international route, between Havana and Key West, and its headquarters in Cuba were at Camp

Columbia, a military airport near Havana. Many of his flights were conducted by Cuban Air Force pilots, and he had no use for bargain fares. A one-way ticket for the ninety-mile trip from Havana to Key West was ten dollars.

Baker reportedly met with Quevada to see if some kind of joint fare could be worked out between cities on National's system and Havana, and the meeting took place over a dinner in Key West.

No common fare was agreed upon, but it is a reasonable assumption that another agreement was reached at this meeting, because, within a very few days after it, Baker applied to the Civil Aeronautics Board for permission to serve Havana from Miami, Tampa, and Key West. His application was strongly supported by the Cuban Government.

Baker yearned for National to become an international carrier. It was about this time that he made his abortive bid to purchase Caribbean-Atlantic Airlines (Caribair) from Dennis Powelson and had his knuckles rapped by the CAB for consummating the deal without Board approval.

"Because of the concurrent Caribair debacle, Baker did not expect to get very far with his application to serve Cuba," a former National executive says, "but here again he was surprised when, in 1946, the CAB granted the certificate to provide service to Havana from the three requested points."

The Cuban equivalent of the CAB quickly granted similar certificates, but only from Tampa and Miami. It never certified National to fly from Havana to Key West in competition with Quevada, and Baker never protested that he was entitled to the route under the bilateral agreement.

There were other American carriers serving Cuba: Pan American out of Miami, and Chicago & Southern (which later was absorbed by Delta). Both of these carriers were paying heavy Cuban taxes because they were foreign corporations operating in Cuba. Primarily to escape these taxes, National set up a separate corporation in Cuba known as Aerovías Internacionales de Cuba. Its basic function was to act as a general agent for National in Cuba, and because it was a domestic operation, its tax rates were much lower than the other American carriers. During the decade and a half that it was in existence, it had more presidents than Cuba itself, which was in conformity with Baker's habit of juggling his executives to keep them off balance. Among the presidents of Aerovías Internacionales were Charles Wilson, Porter Stiles, Robert Weiland, and Cal Kennard. The only person in a managerial capacity who remained with Aerovías Internacionales from its beginning to its end was O. K. (Billy) Williams, a Cuban born in Cienfuegos. Williams was working for Cubana Airlines, the government-owned carrier, and left when National was certified to Havana. He became the airline's station manager but left Havana about a week before the last National flight when he discovered that Castro believed him to be an agent for the Central Intelligence Agency.

The impact of the Cuban expansion upon the airline was strong, particularly at a later date, when the carrier was certified to fly into Havana non-stop from New York. It gave National the prestige of being an American-flag carrier. It made National millions of dollars, and then it cost it millions in later years because Baker attached too much prestige to the role National played as an international carrier with a route that extended only ninety miles outside the continental limits of the United States.

In 1947 New York City turned the operation of La Guardia Airport and the newly constructed Idlewild Airport over to the New York Port Authority. The airlines serving La Guardia were operating under memorandums of understanding, and the costs of operation were extremely low. When the Port Authority took over, it wanted to operate both airports on a paying basis, and the domestic airlines scheduled to start service at Idlewild reacted to the increased costs by boycotting the new airport. At first Baker went along with the boycott, and then for reasons apparently known only to himself, Baker broke the airport boycott and started service out of Idlewild, operating from a hastily thrown-together Quonset-hut-type terminal. The other carriers soon followed National to Idlewild, but because National was the first to inaugurate service, it had first choice for a permanent location for its terminal. There was one exception—the site chosen for the international carriers terminal. One area in this terminal had been set aside for customs and immigration, and when Baker looked at the master plans, it was on this precise section of the international terminal that he placed his finger. Representatives of the New York Port Authority told him it could not be done and recommended that he pick the site chosen by some of his staff.

Baker was adamant. "I am an international carrier," he said, "and I'm going to be in the international terminal. If I don't get it, I'll just sit in my tin shack out there until my lease expires in 1975."

Baker lost the argument. For many years, National lost hundreds of thousands of Miami-bound passengers, who preferred to depart New York from the comfortable and warm terminal of a competitor rather than the drafty, tin terminal complex from which National operated.

The formation of the Cuban company was part of an overall program to identify strongly with the Cuban Government and the people. It was a sound approach. One of the first things that was done was to hire Spanish-speaking stewardesses, all of whom of course were Cuban nationals. It took several months, however, before the United States Department of Immigration would allow the airline to use the girls as stewardesses.

Although by nature Baker was close with the dollar, he was a comparative spendthrift in Cuba. National entertained lavishly. It kept a cabana and rooms in the Hotel Nacional, which was the center of Havana's social life. Everything from poker dice to napkins were donated to every bar and *cantina* in Havana.

For the first few years, on the anniversary date of the inaugural flight, Baker would fly a planeload of social figures and newspapermen from Miami to Havana for an annual party at the Country Club of Havana, which would be attended by most of the prominent figures in Havana's social circles. On one occasion, the party was moved from the Country Club to the American Embassy on the invitation of Ambassador and Mrs. Robert Butler. The dinner was lavish, held in the Embassy garden, and the service was accompanied by strolling musicians. Following the dinner, the guests were treated to a concert by Mrs. Butler, who was known in some circles as the "Hildegarde of the diplomatic corps." While she was entertaining, two of the newsmen drifted out into the foyer of the Embassy.

The Ambassador followed, where he was interviewed in a somewhat hostile manner and quizzed as to who was picking up the bill. The interview reached a point at which Butler had them thrown out of the building. Baker was embarrassed and angry, but he said nothing.

The following year, John Morris once again began planning the anniversary junket. About three days before it was scheduled to take place, Baker called him into his office and told him to cancel it.

"It would be most difficult," Morris replied. "The invitations have gone out and most have been accepted."

For a moment, Baker appeared thoughtful, then he shrugged. "Okay, but this is the last one," he said.

When the group arrived at the Country Club of Havana, Morris was amazed to learn that the dinner had been canceled. On hand were about one hundred fifty civic and political leaders from both Havana and Miami, and the Miami contingent, he knew, had not eaten for several hours. "On whose orders?" he asked.

"Colonel Quevada," he was told.

Morris found the colonel at the end of the bar and drew him aside. "Ted called me," the suave Latin colonel explained with an elaborate shrug. "If a friend asks a favor, you do not question the reason."

Morris quietly slipped from the room, explaining to the maître d'hôtel that there had been a terrible mistake. Within a reasonably short time, tables were set up in an adjacent dining room, and a satisfactory dinner was served. Morris noticed that the only person who picked at his food was Colonel Quevada. Everyone else "was starving."

Baker never mentioned the incident, but a few days after this party he transferred Robert Weiland, who was president of Aerovías Internacionales, to New York. He replaced him with Cal Kennard, who at the time was district sales manager for National in New Orleans.

"I didn't know what he had in mind," Kennard recalls. "He just told me to report to him in Miami, and when I did, he said, 'The tail's been wagging the dog too long in Havana. You are now president of Aerovías Internacionales, and you're going to cut the tail off the dog.'"

Kennard says he felt pretty good about being a president, but after three or four days in Havana he began to "wonder if this was such a good deal or not."

"Baker came down with Jean Brawner, the executive vice president," Kennard recalls. "We had a company car there, a Chevrolet that was about six years old and with about three pistons that were working. I picked up Baker and Brawner at the airport in this car, and before we were halfway into town, Baker was coughing from the smoke seeping up from the floorboards. He told me to get rid of the damn' thing and I agreed with him that a president should be riding around town in something a little better. 'I said get rid of it. I didn't say anything about replacing it.'"

"How am I going to get around, now, Mr. Baker?"

"You can ride the bus."

Kennard wondered about the advantages of being a president when, as a district sales manager, he at least had had an automobile that was only a year old. Kennard never did get rid of the Chevrolet. He had it overhauled and continued to use it. "For a long time after that, every time Baker would come to Havana, he would ask why I hadn't got rid of that car," he says. "I would tell him I was trying to get a good deal on it, and that's where I knew I had him. Baker liked a good deal better than he liked the airline."

The car was still being used as a utility vehicle at the airport as late as 1961.

Baker was most serious, however, about cutting off the wagging tail, and the economy drive was carried to a point where it was impossible to explain to the Cubans, who were well aware that the load factors on National to and from Cuba were higher than they ever had been.

When National first started service to Cuba, its president was Ramón Grau San Martín. He served out his term, which expired in 1948, and was replaced by one of his cabinet ministers, Carlos Prío Socarras, whose term was scheduled to expire in June of 1952. On the morning of March 10, 1952, Batista overthrew Prío as the constitutional president of the republic and once again assumed control of the country. Under both Grau and Prío, even though they were popularly elected presidents, there existed severe currency and travel restrictions, and the overwhelming preponderance of traffic carried in and out of the country was of United States tourists.

Without intending to get into the Cuban political arena, it must be said that Batista removed both these restrictions. He allowed a completely free exchange of travel, and the only currency restriction was a 2% tax on money removed from the country. This attitude benefited all carriers serving Cuba, and particularly National because of its route structure.

During the winter months, the airline ferried North Americans from New York and other areas of the Northeast to the mild-climate, resort atmosphere of Havana. Conversely, during the hot summer months, National was able to carry many middle- and upper-class Cubans from Havana to the cooler resort areas of the Northeast. Cuba was prosperous; there was much money circulation, and it was easy for Cubans to take these vacations. The load factors were high on the airline's planes in both directions consistently throughout the year.

The economy drive in Cuba was clamped on after Baker had lost his bid to acquire Colonial, and became more severe a short time later, when the Civil Aeronautics Board gave Northeast Airlines a temporary five-year certificate to operate in the New York–Florida market. It is apparent that Baker felt there was no need to spend money to promote a flourishing market when he was faced with increased competition on his most profitable domestic route. The economies appeared to be evidence of a penny-pinching attitude rather than of a well-planned program.

Kennard recalls one visit to Havana by Baker that triggered a sequence of events that left Kennard in a state of shock for a week. It started out with a telephone call from Baker's secretary, who reported that her boss was arriving for an inspection tour the following morning and would be returning to Miami that same afternoon. No sooner had Baker's secretary hung up than Kennard received a call from Walter Sternberg, National's vice president of sales. Five of National's top accounts would be arriving in Havana on the following day, and would Mr. Kennard please arrange to take them to the Kid Gavilán-Billy Graham fight, which was scheduled to be held in Havana that evening. Although ringside fight seats were selling for seventy-five dollars, Mr. Sternberg would authorize the expenditure.

On the following morning, Kennard met Baker at the airport and, among other things, Baker wanted to see the cargo area. Among the piles of cartons was a plywood cage, with a corrugated metal door, that contained a cat. The animal had been flown to Havana from New York. It was scheduled to be picked up by another carrier and flown on to Panamá late in the afternoon. Baker looked at the shipping label and then at the crate.

"We rent these cages, and we are supposed to get them

back," he said to Kennard. "Now you know damn' well we'll never get that cage back from Panamá. When all that's involved is a cat or a small dog, it would be better to sell the shipper a small cage made out of that heavy corrugated cardboard rather than throw away an expensive one like this."

"Yes sirrr, Mr. Baker," Kennard replied. "We'll do that in the future."

The two men finished their tour of the airport facilities and drove to the downtown offices of Aerovías Internacionales.

"While we were talking after lunch," Kennard recalls, "one of the girls from the office came in and asked me to sign the check for five hundred dollars for the fight tickets. It wasn't very good timing on the part of that little girl. Ted Baker reacted like he had just lost five hundred round-trip fares to New York. He picked up the telephone and called Sternberg. This was an overseas call, remember, and it probably cost a hundred dollars to find out why Sternberg wanted to have me take five guys to a fight, but Sternberg finally convinced him.

"Baker then said he had a connection and he would buy the tickets. He was gone for about an hour, and when he came back he was soaking wet. There had been a very heavy thundershower. But Baker had six tickets, all ringside, to the fight, and he told me he had only paid fifty dollars each for them and so he had saved a hundred and twenty-five dollars. I remember he told me he had sent me down to cut off that wagging tail and some of it was still wagging."

In the late afternoon, Kennard drove Baker out to the airport and saw him off on the Miami flight. A few hours later, he picked up his guests at the Hotel Nacional and drove them over to the stadium where the fight was being held.

"When we reached our seats, we found them occupied by a group of Cuban gentlemen who indicated that they had no intention of giving them up. I must admit that they had some justification for this attitude because they also had tickets to the same seats. Within a very few minutes, we were attracting more attention at the ringside seats than the preliminary fight going on in the ring. First came a battalion of ushers and behind them a battalion of cops. I had a hundred and fifty dollars in my pocket and it took every penny of it to get everyone calmed down and get a row of folding chairs set up so close to the ring that the only part of the fight we could see was when Kid Gavilán once leaned over the ropes."

The following afternoon, Kennard received a telephone call from Billy Williams at the airport. "That was a very valuable cat," Billy said.

"What cat?"

It was an extraordinarily expensive cat with a Siamese background, which probably accounted for its being named Bangkok. It belonged to the wife of an admiral who was stationed in Panamá, and it had won ribbons and prizes and cups from one end of the United States to the other. Someone in the Canal Zone had decided to put on a cat show, and the wife of the admiral had decided to enter Bangkok in the competition. Bangkok had been staying with relatives in Washington and had been shipped via National to Havana for transshipment to Panamá on another carrier.

Kennard sighed. "This is the cat that drew Mr. Baker's attention yesterday?"

It was indeed the same cat. One of the cargo managers had acted upon Mr. Baker's suggestion and had transferred Bangkok from the wooden cage to a cheaper, corrugated-cardboard cage and then had placed it outside the door of the cargo storage area for pickup by the other carrier. "Do you remember that rainstorm we had yesterday?" Williams asked.

Kennard remembered the rainstorm.

After the cage had collapsed in the downpour, Bangkok had stepped out and disappeared. When his absence was noticed, a search was launched immediately, with cargo personnel crying out alternately for Bangkok and Kitty in coaxing tones. Although the cat's name caused certain ribald remarks from other workers around the airport, it paid off when a feline came purring out from behind an assortment of crates. The cat was safely installed in another cardboard cage and sent on its way. The more expensive, wooden cage was sent back to New York.

Again Cal Kennard sighed. "I'm glad that one was straightened out," he said.

"Well, not quite," Williams told him reluctantly. "The admiral's wife is upset. It seems that the cat that was sent on to Panamá was not Bangkok. It was one of the alley cats that prowled around the cargo area."

No one ever found Bangkok. No one seems to recall how much was paid to the admiral's wife in settlement for Bangkok's freedom. Today, Kennard is the airline's district sales manager in San Francisco, and whenever he receives a memo from the general office referring to economy, he shudders and recalls Baker's six-hour foray through Havana in search of economy.

Until the latter part of the fifties it was Cuba that kept National financially healthy. There were minor route extensions—a certification westward to Houston in 1956 and north to Providence and Boston in the following year. The peak year for profits for the airline was 1956, when National netted $4.3 million, and the greatest percentage of this profit came from the Cuban run. The following year, Cuba was becoming known as a troubled nation as the Castro forces grew stronger and cautious tourists began to bypass Havana as a resort area. National's net profit dipped to $3 million.

In the fall of 1958, Baker went to Havana for a meeting with Burke Hedges, a man with large financial interests in Cuba and a member of the Board of Aerovías Internacionales. Although Hedges had been born in the United States, he later became a citizen of Cuba, then a senator, and at the time of this meeting with Baker, Hedges was the Cuban ambassador to Brazil.

Baker reported that Hedges had told him that Batista could pick up Fidel Castro any time he wanted to, but that he was reluctant to make a martyr of him and that he did not consider him a very serious threat to the government. Hedges reportedly told Baker also, however, that he thought the Batista government was riddled with Castro supporters and that the ruling hierarchy was overly complacent. The revolution stands a good chance of succeeding, Hedges said.

A short time after this meeting, National's flight 402, an Electra turboprop, had just turned away from the Havana terminal when the building was rocked by an explosion and fire. The aircraft was full, and if the explosion had occurred a few minutes earlier, the plane probably would have been destroyed, with resulting casualties to all on board. This was the last Electra to fly on scheduled service into Havana until the inauguration of the so-called Freedom Flights many years later. Service was continued to Havana with DC-7 and DC-6 piston equipment for several months, but at diminishing frequency. The loads were mostly empty going in, full coming out.

Early on New Year's Day, in 1959, Baker was awakened at his home by a telephone call from his old friend Colonel Manuel Quevada. The colonel was in Jacksonville, Florida, where he had landed after flying Batista and other members of the government out of the country. "Why don't you apply for that Key West–Havana run now, Ted?" he said. "I have suspended service."

Charles (Buck) Wilson, the last president of Aerovías Internacionales, heard the news by telephone from Miami very early in the morning on New Year's Day of 1959. He tried to reach Billy Williams by telephone but could not get through. The overseas calls were working perfectly, but it was impossible to place a local call. He drove to Williams' home, awakened him, and told him "Batista has blown, and we've got a problem."

Both men drove immediately to the airport. The terminal was packed with refugees, most of them minor officials of the Batista government willing to go anywhere so long as it was out of Cuba. There were many members of the Batista police in evidence, but most of them leaned against the walls and did nothing either to help or to hinder the refugees. Later in the morning, however, a sergeant approached Williams and proposed that they shake down some of the upper-middle-class refugees.

"When you recognize some big shot trying to slip out of the country," the sergeant said, "refer them to me. We will split whatever I get and there should be some worth a couple of thousand dollars."

Williams knew better than to disagree with a police sergeant, so he merely nodded and turned away. He referred no one to the police sergeant. About an hour later, the first of the Castro forces began to appear at the airport, and the police sergeant himself became a refugee dressed in civilian clothes and boarded a Pan Am flight for Miami.

By eleven in the morning, all the early flights had been dispatched, loaded to capacity. There were two aircraft on the ground. One was scheduled to depart at 11:50 and the other at 3 p.m. By eleven, the Castro forces had seized control of the Department of Immigration and ordered all the carriers to refuse passage to anyone who was a citizen of Cuba. Two men, dressed in civilian clothes and brandishing pistols, searched the flight that was scheduled to depart at 11:50 and forcibly removed more than a dozen Cuban nationals. Their places were quickly taken by frightened tourists. Ten minutes before this flight departed, a member of the porters' union came to Williams' office and told him that at noon the airport was going to be closed down for at least a week.

Williams raced around the airport rounding up the crew, and at three minutes before noon the DC-7 lifted off the runway. It was the last foreign-flag carrier to get out of Havana for five days.

By midafternoon on the first, the Castro forces had taken control of the airport. None of these were *campesinos*. They were young people, very polite and civilized, Williams recalls, and many were either professional men or government officials who had been working at the airport but had not been known to be supporters of Castro. However, within the next two or three days, they were slowly replaced by the tougher element of the Castro movement, the young *barbudos,* the illiterates and the peasants who had been with Castro in the hills. These carbine-carrying guards, the *campesinos,* refused to let anyone in or out of the airport without a special pass.

"These passes were issued by a man who was designated as being in charge of the airport," Williams says, "but no one knew who he was or where he had located his offices. I could not call out to Miami by now, but Miami could call me. It was very difficult to explain that there was an airport manager, but I didn't know who he was or where his offices were located, or have any idea when, if ever, service would be resumed."

The mysterious airport manager lasted about a week, then abruptly disappeared. There was nothing mysterious about the new airport manager. He was a young lieutenant named Mateos, a *barbudo,* who had been with Castro in the hills, and now, according to the credentials he showed Williams and Wilson, he was a member of the Cuban Army's G-2 staff.

"Mateos was very polite, somewhat fearful, and he would listen attentively to all of the problems brought before him in the ensuing months by the various airlines," Williams says. "However, he only knew one word—'no.' No matter what the problem, what the emergency, Mateos always said 'no.'"

When the airport was reopened, National resumed service. For a while, the loads coming into Cuba were extraordinarily heavy, consisting primarily of Cuban exiles who had fled the Batista regime. Then this inbound traffic halted abruptly following the mass executions in Havana by Castro. The absolute ban on outbound travel had been lifted, and presently the traffic flow reversed itself again.

National's first daily departure from Havana was at 10 a.m. Very quickly Williams learned that if there was to be any chance to get the flight out on schedule, he was required to be at the airport before 6 a.m.

The fleeing Cubans carried an incredible amount of baggage. Williams remembers one morning, about 6:30, when a middle-aged gentleman came to the counter and asked permission to check in his luggage.

"Of course."

The passenger called for several porters and went out to a truck, and Williams stared in amazement as the man's "baggage" was unloaded. "He had about four dozen 'Cuban duffel bags,' each weighing about one hundred pounds, and two large beds."

This man was lucky and got out with all of his baggage. Many other passengers were not so fortunate. By now, passengers leaving Cuba were required by government law to check in at least two hours before flight time. After the flight was entirely checked in, manifests went to the various departments of the Cuban Government that had mushroomed over the airport. Each department apparently had its own list of "suspects." Williams was required to prepare twenty-three copies of the manifest, one for each department at the airport. Each department would pick out a few persons and order them brought to him with all of their luggage. A passenger could be subjected to a dozen interrogations before he was allowed to board the plane. Sometimes these inquiries would last hours, and planes were not allowed to depart until all the interrogations were concluded.

Unlike the previous regimes, it was impossible to speed the process by tips or a bribe. "Everyone under the Castro administration was thoroughly honest," Williams says. "It was not honesty for the sake of honesty; it was because everyone had grown accustomed to the practice of informing on everyone else."

It was common practice for men and women to be stripped and searched. A particularly attractive female might be required to remove her clothes a half dozen times between check-in and plane boarding. Most of the harassment was directed toward Cubans, but the few tourists that did come in received no special privileges.

There was not a penny's profit in serving Cuba. The aircraft flew down empty, and although they came back full, none of the money paid for the tickets came into National's possession. A Castro edict required that any Cuban who wished to depart to the United States must purchase his ticket with United States dollars. If the ticket was purchased in the United States, National was required by law to deposit an equal sum in the Bank of Cuba. No money could be removed from the country.

Baker made one attempt to get around the restriction by entering the cigar business. He bought five thousand expensive Cuban cigars with the frozen funds, but they were confiscated at the airport by the Cuban Department of Customs. Thereafter, Baker would complain, "They're my goddam cigars," whenever he saw a picture of Castro puffing away.

By the end of fiscal 1960, National's financial sheet showed a loss of $2.9 million, of which a large portion could be attributed directly to the disintegration of the Cuban market. By the fall of 1960, Baker knew that, if the airline was to survive, it would have to suspend its service entirely to Havana.

Shortly after Labor Day, National quietly began to move its equipment out of Cuba. First went ground-support equipment, then spare parts for the aircraft, all loaded on the aircraft in small enough quantities to escape attention.

Unknown to Baker, and to Williams and Wilson also, there was another type of smuggling going on—refugees. Working in the air cargo department was a young man named Abdul Soliva who had come to Cuba from Lebanon shortly after the end of World War II. He had no political or nationalistic ties, but he did have a strong empathy for refugees. The word soon spread around the anti-Castro underground that, if it was a matter of life or death, Soliva could get a person out of Cuba.

Soliva's operation was a simple one. He merely checked recent manifests for names of United States citizens who had departed Cuba a week or ten days earlier. He substituted these names for those of the refugees who wished to leave, and filled out the proper landing tourist cards and other documents required by the government. He had discovered that the Cuban bureaucrats would check to see if such a person had entered Cuba, but never thought of checking to see if he had departed on an earlier date.

The North American citizens usually were segregated from Cuban nationals at check-in and taken immediately on board the aircraft, which was air conditioned.

Eventually, word of Soliva's operation reached the police via the informer system, and he was picked up for questioning, held for several hours, then released. A day or so later, he noticed the same two police officers who had arrested him earlier drive up to the air cargo department. "I'm just going to lunch," he told one of his co-workers, and he strolled out of the building. A few minutes later he was safely hidden in a lavatory of a plane leaving for Miami. The police still were searching Havana for Soliva hours after he had landed safely in Miami.

By January of 1961, National's service to Cuba consisted of one flight a week. Then President Eisenhower issued his dictum that any person going to Cuba from the United States must have special permission from the U. S. State Department. When this ruling was announced, both Williams and Wilson were in Miami. National's payroll in Cuba had dwindled to less than fifteen persons. Castro became convinced that the only persons the U. S. State Department would allow to visit Cuba would be agents for the Central Intelligence Agency. Neither Williams nor Wilson went back. National's service to Havana was suspended.

There is a story that eight hundred thousand dollars in

cash was left behind by the airline in the Bank of Cuba. Most evidence points to the truth of the story, but left behind also were the books of Aerovías Internacionales, as was the old Chevrolet that had once provided transportation for Aerovías president Cal Kennard.

Although service to Havana now has been suspended for the better part of a decade, the mark of Cuba still is visible upon the airline. National became strongly identified with Cuba, not only because it gave the airline its greatest source of revenue, but because it also was its only international route. A large number of its Cuban employees still work for the airline. One former stewardess now has a daughter flying for the carrier. In virtually every station there are Cubans working for the airline, many of them in managerial capacity and of long tenure. Few, if any, have any desire to return to Cuba, even if Castro were overthrown.

When Billy Williams moved permanently to the United States, in 1961, his son was ten and his daughter seven. "Now, to them, Cuba is a strange country where they spent some of their childhood. They speak Spanish with an accent and English with no accent. They don't want any of it. And the younger generation in Cuba, too, has changed. They have been taught to hate the United States, and it would take decades to erase it. It is unlikely that we will ever go back," Williams says, "yet, to me, National is a sort of Cuban airline. I think of it as a part of Aerovías Internacionales, and there are many of us with this feeling."

Baker did not decry the loss of Havana from any sentimental reasons. It was one of three reasons why National was facing a record loss of $7¼ million. The other two reasons were the jet-acquisition costs and the introduction of Northeast Airlines into the New York–Florida market.

Baker knew that his only hope for survival was to be awarded a good portion of the Southern Transcontinental Route, which was due for decision by the Civil Aeronautics

Board in approximately sixty days. He knew also, however, that National had not been given a significant route for more than fifteen years, and, in case he missed out on this, he had already made preliminary plans to merge National with Continental.

CHAPTER ELEVEN

The profit on the sale of Frontier was $1.8 million for four years of work. The price that Baker had asked for sale of the control of National was thirty-five dollars per share, but Bud Maytag assumed that this was not necessarily a firm price. If it was, he was in trouble. Maytag knew that he could borrow enough to meet this price, but he knew also that the interest on this kind of money "will eat you up."

There was a young man in New York named G. Robert Truex, a gregarious, affable, and soft-spoken banker who was a vice president of the Irving Trust Company. Maytag and Truex were close friends and had enjoyed also a close financial relationship during Maytag's operation of Frontier.

There is little about Truex that suggests the image of a banker, and he says that he got into the business by accident. He is a native of Red Bank, New Jersey, and spent most of his childhood there. When he was graduated from college, "I made the rounds of the employment agencies in New York, and one of them sent me to the Irving Trust Company.

"I liked the people I met there and I thought frankly that the opportunities were greater in the commercial banking business because they didn't have a lot of guys like me pushing to get to the top spots in them. It was the lowest financial offer I had, but it was the one I took."

He has a chameleon's ability to adapt to his environment and to people, and this probably accounts for the fact that he is liked immediately by everyone from little old ladies in lace to the roughest teamster. It probably contributes partially also to his meteoric rise in the banking industry to where he is now, executive vice president of the Bank of America. He has never fallen into the patronizing syndrome associated with so many bankers, and this, too, may be a clue to his success.

Several years ago, when he was in New York, he looked up from his desk one afternoon to see an elderly Chinese peering at him over the railing. The man's topcoat showed the first signs of wear, and his hat obviously had been around for a few years. Truex invited the man inside the railing and did not blink an eye when the customer indicated he wanted a short-term loan of four million dollars. Instead of brushing away the man as a crank, Truex continued to listen to him, then discovered that in spite of his sweat-stained hat and threadbare overcoat the Chinese was a multimillionaire with blue-chip credit, and that such a loan would eagerly be solicited by any bank in the United States.

Later, Truex learned that his customer, who lived in a subtropical area of the United States, came to New York so infrequently that he had not considered it a good investment to buy a hat and a coat, so he had borrowed this equipment from a friend. Before reaching the Irving Trust, the man had been to four other banks in New York and been shunted away before he could identify himself or state the reason for his visit.

It is highly improbable that Bud Maytag ever wore a threadbare overcoat or a sweat-stained hat, but there is a parallel in his relationship with Truex.

"When we first went into Frontier, it was virtually broke," Maytag recalls. "No one would touch it. Of course, bankers were calling on us all the time, but when they saw the picture, they quickly lost interest. Then one day Bob Truex came in. We had mutual friends in Denver, and I had dinner with him. As a result of this and subsequent meetings, Bob Truex finally convinced his people back in New York to grant us a loan.

Our friendship started before the loan, but in addition to our personal relationship, I felt obligated to him, and when the National venture first arose, Bob Truex was kept informed and invited to become a member of the board of directors if the deal with Baker was consummated."

Thus, very shortly after the discussion with Baker, Maytag had another discussion with Truex.

"Bud thought he could make a deal for about $6,400,000," Truex says. "He knew that he could borrow this money, but the interest would eat him alive. His alternative was to have someone go in with him. I told him I knew of a man who had money and certainly was interested in the airlines and who might be interested in going in with Bud on National. This man was Dudley Swim.

"He didn't know Dudley, but I knew Dudley fairly well. I knew that Dudley had been a transportation buff all his life. He had been interested in the railroads in their heyday and had transferred this affection to the airlines when they began to move into prominence. At this time, he was a large stockholder in Western Airlines and also a director.

"I told Bud about him, and Bud was very interested. I then called Dudley and told him what the situation was in reference to National and what a fine guy Bud was—that there was no question of his integrity or ability or anything else. At this time, Dudley was a director of Investors Diversified Services in Minneapolis. He said he had a meeting coming up in Minneapolis, that he could arrange his trip so that he could lay over in Denver for thirty or forty minutes, and that he would be delighted to talk to him if Mr. Maytag could be at the airport."

The date of the meeting was set for the following day.

Maytag called in Woody; Ed Dolansky, his vice president of finance; Bill Nelson, his legal vice president; and Dan Brock, his vice president of sales and traffic. "We burned the midnight oil that night," Maytag recalls. "Although we had analyzed National thoroughly, broken out the areas that we believed to be deficient and what was wrong with it, it still had to be put in a more presentable form for a stranger like Swim to understand it.

"I met Swim at the airport, a most pleasant and charming man. We talked about National for about ten minutes. Then he changed the subject and began discussing the industry in general. Then, a few minutes before the plane left, he said casually that he would be interested in going in with me. I couldn't believe it. He didn't know me, and as far as I knew, he didn't know National."

When Truex called Swim, he was the largest stockholder on the board of directors of Western Airlines. It was not a large position in terms of dollars, because the Western board was not heavy on stockholdings.

Apparently unknown to both Truex and Maytag, he knew National and had had some indirect financial dealings with Baker in 1950, through Investors Diversified Services. National's stock at that time had been selling for around fifteen dollars a share, and either Baker, or Lehman Brothers acting on his behalf, had made a private placement with Investors Diversified for one hundred thousand shares.

"There was some concern and worry about the investment," Swim recalls, "because Baker was not fully understood. It was a situation of continuing concern. Baker was an unorthodox person, but he was resourceful."

Thus, when Truex called Swim and told him Maytag was looking for an associate to buy into a major airline, National, Swim had some familiarity with the carrier.

"I immediately liked Bud Maytag and I believed in the industry," Swim says. "National had recently been awarded the Southern Transcontinental Route (which extended it from Houston through Nevada into California), and the plan made sense to me. My investment decisions usually are made on the basis of a few broad fundamentals. I don't have to grind through a lot of statistics."

Swim says the decision to buy into National posed no problem for him. It took no time at all for him to come to a "yes" conclusion. "I was in the airline business and National had received the award for the Southern Transcontinental Route."

Swim is an urbane, sophisticated man in his early sixties who occasionally refers to himself as "a country boy at heart." This reference undoubtedly refers to his birth in the small and inauspicious town of Bellingham, Washington, and his boyhood in Twin Falls, Idaho. He attended Stanford University and then moved to Wall Street, where he "went through the deluge" of the 1929 crash. Since that time, he has parlayed a small investment in transportation companies and mutual funds into an estate estimated at $100 million today.

In some circles he is considered a man of mystery, but this is caused by an innate shyness toward publicity. There is nothing shy about Swim, however, when he is around people. Here, he exudes a charm that contradicts any characteristics of a shy man. Swim kept out of the preliminary negotiations to buy National. He had made a commitment to Bud Maytag, but this was predicated upon the consummation of the deal.

The preliminary negotiations were conducted in a small suite in the International Hotel, located in the terminal building at the Miami Airport. Present were John Love, John Cross, Bud Maytag, and Ted Baker.

The meeting should have been one charged with emotion and suspense. To Baker it signified the ending of his career, if the transaction was completed. To Maytag it meant winning a long-odds gamble upon which he literally was betting his last penny. Yet the meeting is remembered as "rather casual and matter-of-fact" by those who attended.

Maytag was the last to arrive. He accepted a cup of coffee, then walked over to the soundproofed window overlooking the terminal loading areas and watched the planes as Baker finished telling a story about William Pawley. Some years earlier, Pawley had chartered a Lodestar in Washintgon for a flight to New York. On board the plane, in addition to Pawley, were Baker and Kershaw. As it approached New York, the aircraft ran into bad weather, and the airports were forced to close down. For almost two hours Kershaw circled around New York waiting for a "break," and then, as the fuel became low, Pawley suggested that they ditch it in the Hudson River. Baker became indignant. The plane was worth fifty thousand dollars. I'll buy the goddam plane, Pawley retorted. Just ditch it. Baker went on to say that Kershaw finally put the plane down at Newark and that, once the wheels touched the runway, Pawley withdrew his offer.

Maytag laughed politely and at the same time wondered if Baker's purpose in telling the story was to indicate that the sale was off. Maytag placed his coffee cup on the window sill and turned around. Baker was sitting on a sofa behind a large coffee table on which there was a yellow pad of legal-sized paper. "I can come up with twenty dollars a share," Maytag said aloud. He expected Baker to throw up his hands and walk out of the room.

Baker, however, only leaned forward slightly and drummed his finger softly on the coffee table. "We were talking about thirty to thirty-five dollars a share," he replied mildly.

Maytag shrugged slightly. "That's all the money I can raise. Six million for two hundred fifty thousand shares."

Baker took a pen from his pocket and scribbled on the paper. No one in the room said a word, the only sound the soft whirring of the air-conditioning unit. Baker leaned back and stared at the ceiling. "Will you split the difference?" he asked.

Maytag sighed slowly to cover a surge of elation. He knew now that he had it. It really was the first indication that Baker had given that he really was prepared to sell.

"Another half million," Baker said softly.

"I don't know, Ted. This is all the money I've been able to scrape up, but I'll check with my people." He left the suite and went to his own room, which was on the same floor of the hotel. He called Dudley Swim in Carmel, California. Swim agreed to go in for between 10 and 20% above the market price. It would be on a fifty-fifty basis. Maytag knew that if he "got into trouble" he could sell Swim a hundred thousand shares for around eighteen dollars.

Maytag returned to the suite. "I can go another four hundred thousand, Ted, and that's it. That's all I can raise."

This time, Baker did not hesitate. "It's a deal." He turned to John Cross. "Write it up on one page, John," he said. He wanted one condition attached to the sale—the rights of first refusal to purchase the stock should Maytag offer it for sale. Maytag agreed, with one exception. He reserved the right to make one sale of stock within the first sixty days. Baker had no objection. He rose from the sofa saying he would be available in his offices in the WPST Building if there were any further questions. Maytag wondered why Baker still maintained an office in his defunct television station, but he did not ask.

The stories and opinions involving the "Channel 10 case" are contradictory and diverse, but there is agreement and testimony that it did cost National two major route extensions.

There is agreement also that the idea of diversifying into television came from Robert Foreman, National's corporate secretary.

The answer as to what really occurred with the Channel 10 imbroglio probably will never be known. All the principals involved in the bitter fight are dead, with one exception, and the exception is in such a position that it is unlikely he will discuss it.

There were four contestants for the Channel 10 license in Miami: National Airlines, with George Baker as president; a Miami Beach attorney named A. Frank Katzentine, who owned Radio Station WKAT; L. B. Wilson, Inc., which operated a string of hillbilly radio stations; and North Dade Video Inc., which probably was the smartest of all the applicants, in that it bowed out gracefully long before the first handful of mud was thrown.

The hearings on the case were opened on January 29, 1954. On February 8, 1957, the FCC awarded the license to National Airlines by a four-to-two vote, reversing the recommendation of a hearing officer that the license be given to Katzentine. The chairman of the FCC at this time was Richard A. Mack of Miami, and Mack voted in favor of National.

On August 1, 1957, National's television station, operating as WPST-TV, went on the air.

Less than six months later, in January of 1958, the tent flaps were pulled back to open another Washington circus, and Channel 10 was in the middle ring. The opening act was a public hearing on the FCC held by the House Subcommittee on Legislative Oversight, and Chief Counsel Schwartz set the scene when he announced that powerful persons were involved in the Channel 10 case. Two weeks later, Schwartz was fired by the subcommittee. Next, Committee Chairman Morgan Moulder of Missouri resigned in protest over the firing of Schwartz and was replaced by Representative Oren Harris of Arkansas.

Schwartz next appeared as a witness before the committee and testified that Mack had received $2,650 from Miami Attorney Thurmond Whiteside, who allegedly represented National Airlines. Schwartz claimed that Mack had pledged his vote to National. Then, turning on Katzentine, Schwartz said that the Miami Beach attorney also had tried to influence Mack through former Miami Mayor Perrine Palmer and Jerry Carter, a Florida Railroad Commission member. Schwartz also testified that Katzentine also sought an ally in Senator George Smathers.

When Whiteside reached the stand in late February, he testified that he had given Mack some thirteen thousand dollars from outside mutual business interests and that Mack was part owner of an agency that handled insurance for Channel 10. Katzentine testified that Baker had wielded improper influence. Mack was excoriated by the committee when he took the stand, and a few days later, he resigned. The investigation then started to turn toward the White House, and on March 17, an angry George Gordon Moore, Mamie Eisenhower's brother-in-law, refuted charges that he had asked for or received government favors in the case. Six days later, the investigation was closed.

In the ensuing months, both Mack and Whiteside were indicted by a federal grand jury. Whiteside committed suicide. Mack died a short time later. The FCC began another investigation and eventually revoked the license it had issued to National, spurned Katzentine, and gave it to L. B. Wilson. When Wilson died, Senator George Smathers, who since has retired from the Senate, became trustee for the estate and thus, for all practical purposes, the affairs of Channel 10 came under his direction.

Foreman says the idea for diversifying into television came up during a casual conversation with Baker on an entirely different matter. "I said to him, why in hell don't we apply for a television channel. We have all these communications guys, radio guys, and they could put the thing together for next to nothing."

A few weeks later, according to Foreman, Cy Lewis, a member of National's board of directors, was in Miami and mentioned to Baker that he had made a lot of money by investing in a St. Louis television station. It was this comment that started Baker in his last-minute rush to seek the license for Channel 10 before the deadline some three days thence. Foreman contends also that Katzentine triggered the investigation through his friendship with the late Senator Estes Kefauver.

"Whenever Kefauver came to Miami, he stayed at Katzentine's house," Foreman says, "and it was Kefauver that got the ball rolling."

Those who were closest to Baker are vehement in their denials that Baker acquired his television license through any form of trickery or fraud. "They crucified my husband," says his widow. "They crucified him in this case, and it was not justified."

Lou Bower says that, from the first, Baker seemed to be bewildered by the developments in the Channel 10 case. "I think this is what killed him," Bower says.

Baker probably was a victim of the political climate of the time. A considerable outcry was made over the fact that the FCC had overruled its own hearing officer to grant Baker the license. This is a moot point. Hearing officers often are overruled by the Commission, as are examiners' recommendations often overruled by the Civil Aeronautics Board. The same situation exists in other phases of the regulatory arms of government.

The improper influence that Baker was alleged to have wielded upon the Commission through Mack makes no sense for two reasons. First, the Commission had already overruled the hearing officer before Mack was appointed to the Commission. Second, the FCC vote to award the channel to National was recorded as four in favor and two against. Had Mack abstained, the license still would have been awarded to National. That Whiteside knew Mack well, however, that they had mutual business interests, cannot be refuted, and probably this is the reason that Whiteside suddenly became a specialist in FCC matters.

Retired generals, for example, often are hired as specialists or consultants at large salaries by companies whose business depends upon the award of military contracts. In such cases, "consultant" or "specialist" is but a euphemism for a man who has the "contacts" with the Pentagon. Without such "contacts," the problems of doing business with any arm of the government become much more difficult. This does not mean that there is any unethical procedure either by the specialist or the arm of the government in which he is an expert. Prior to a recent election in Los Angeles, a volunteer worker brought a press release concerning his candidate's activity into a metropolitan newspaper and left it on the somewhat cluttered desk of one of the sports editors, where it was found the day after the election. A specialist would have taken it to the political editor. Baker wanted a specialist in FCC matters, and in this category he retained Whiteside.

Even some of Baker's strongest critics think he was a political victim in the Channel 10 case. "He had an expression he would use once in a great while," a former National executive recalls. "If you steal a chicken, you don't pluck it on the way home." (Baker's boyhood experience at Pullman, Michigan, apparently never was forgotten.)

"If Ted Baker had ever bought anyone off in the FCC, there could have been no way anyone ever could have found out about it."

The big loss to National, however, was not the Miami television station. It was the loss of the routes for which it had been recommended by a CAB examiner from Chicago to Miami and from St. Louis to Miami. Running almost concurrently with the FCC hearings over the Channel 10 award were the oral arguments in the route extensions to Chicago and St. Louis.

"How can one arm of the government reward a carrier which is under investigation by another arm of the government?" an attorney for another airline asked.

The CAB apparently thought that this indeed would be a matter subject to criticism and awarded the routes to Northwest Orient and TWA.

CHAPTER TWELVE

Baker was too busy to stay and work out the details of the sale. The moment the agreement was reached orally, he stood up, went to the door, turned and again admonished Cross to keep the agreement to one page, then went out the door.

Maytag, Cross, and Love went to the office of another attorney, Paul Scott, in downtown Miami. For two days, the four men worked over the conditions of the sale, and when they were done, the contract was ten pages long.

"We took it back to Ted and he wouldn't even read it," Maytag recalls wryly. "He said, 'I haven't got the time to read this. Put it on one page. Put it on one page or the hell with the deal.' "

There was no reason why Baker should not be humored, Maytag decided, no reason other than six and a half million dollars. Nevertheless, Maytag did humor him and went back to Scott's office, where another two days were spent in shrinking the contract. No matter now they tried, however, the best that could be done was a contract three pages long. Again the three lawyers and Maytag returned to Baker's office.

Baker was almost petulant. "I said to put it on one page."

John Cross was gentle. "Ted," he said quietly, "for two million dollars a page, don't you have time to read three pages?"

Baker sighed and picked up the papers. He read them carefully. "Is this all right with you, John?" he asked.

Cross nodded, and Baker picked up his pen and scribbled his name across the bottom of the last page.

Also to be signed were several letters of agreement that were attachments to the contract, and these letters filled in the other conditions of the bill of sale. One of these agreements gave Baker the right of first refusal on resale of the stock except that there could be one transaction within sixty days, which would be exempt. This was the block of stock that was to go to Dudley Swim, although Swim's name was not mentioned. From remarks Baker made later, he assumed that a portion of the stock was to be transferred to another member of the Maytag family.

Another letter of attachment was an agreement to pay Baker thirty thousand dollars annually as a consultant and to keep him on the board of directors.

The closing of the sale of National Airlines took place in the board room of the First National Bank of Miami. Among those present were Ted and Irma Baker, Bob Truex, a collection of attorneys, and Bud Maytag. The stock certificates were brought in and placed in front of Baker. Baker looked at them casually, then glanced up toward the ceiling.

"If you will endorse those," one of the lawyers suggested after a while.

"I'm not signing anything," Baker replied.

Maytag sighed.

"I'll sign them after I get paid," Baker added presently.

Again Maytag sighed, took the certified check from his briefcase, and slid it along the table. "I was nervous every minute," Maytag recalls. "I still didn't know whether I had a deal or not, and I wouldn't know until I had those signed stock certificates in my possession."

Baker picked up the check and studied it carefully. Then, after a long pause, he began signing the certificates.

"Even then he seemed skittish," Maytag says, "but from then on, everything went off smoothly. He signed them all.

He gave me a key. I never have found out what lock it fit, but he gave me a key, and that was that."

Bob Truex remembers a brief conversation he had had with the beautiful Irma Baker just before the meeting took place. She had remarked that she loved to wear hats and that she loved to go to New York because it gave her the chance, but that she never wore them in Miami. Truex says, "When Bud passed Ted the check for $6.4 million the thought that flickered through my mind was that that could buy Mrs. Baker one hell of a hat."

Irma Baker has yet another memory. "When we came out of the bank after we had deposited this huge check, I had to go somewhere, which would leave Ted without transportation. He was going to the offices of Channel 10, and I suggested he take a cab. Instead he took the bus. Here he had just deposited this huge check, and he took a bus."

Any thought Baker may have had he kept to himself.

The first person at National Airlines to learn of the sale, other than Baker, was Lew Dymond, the vice president of flight operations. Dymond went to work for the airline shortly after Baker started operations out of Jacksonville and worked his way from the equivalent of a ground attendant up through the ranks to an airline presidency. Along the way, he had picked up a degree in law and had learned to fly.

Although he often fought with Baker, he had a strong affection for him, and this feeling was reciprocated by Baker. Dymond often was a guest at the Bakers' home on Bay Point in Miami. He knew that Baker's health was not good, and he knew also that Irma Baker wanted her husband to take up a more relaxing manner of life because of his health.

There are conflicting stories about a dinner at the Baker home in the summer of 1961. Lew Dymond and Lou Bower were present, and both recall Baker saying casually that he had been given a $100,000 option check for his holdings in National, but that he did not think anything would come of it, because "the guy has to get rid of an airline first." Irma Baker does not remember such a conversation, and, of course, Baker had not taken any money from Maytag. Such a conversation, however, could easily explain Dymond's actions following an incredible coincidence that occurred some months later.

Early in the following April, while Maytag was gathering up the necessary funds to purchase control of National, Dymond was called to New York to attend a meeting of the New York Port Authority. While checking in for the flight, he saw Mrs. Richard Pistell, whom he had met socially in Miami, and she introduced him to her husband, whom she was seeing off to New York. Because of this introduction, Dymond and Pistell sat together on the flight. About a half hour after the plane was airborne, Pistell mentioned casually that he had purchased an airline and that he needed someone to run it. During the ensuing conversation and before the plane landed at Newark, Pistell had offered the presidency of Frontier to Dymond. The offer was not immediately accepted.

After Dymond left Pistell in New York, he suddenly remembered the conversation with Baker that had taken place the previous summer. By the time Dymond returned to Miami, he was convinced that Baker had been telling the truth and that Maytag was the man who had made the offer. He went to Baker immediately and challenged him. Baker confirmed his suspicions and Dymond then told him that he had been offered the presidency of Frontier.

"Baker didn't want me to leave," Dymond says. "He said it was a mistake, that Frontier would not last very long, and that Maytag would need me. I replied, 'You may know that and I may know that, but does Bud Maytag know it?' Baker then said that he wasn't sure that Maytag was going to take the option. The conversation took place at Baker's house on a Sunday afternoon, two days before I accepted Pistell's offer and came to Denver. I remember telling him that I didn't think he should sell National, but he replied that he was going to sell it."

Many of the older employees at National, particularly those in the executive ranks, believe that Baker "took care of Dymond" as a part of the transaction, but this is not true. Frontier has since changed ownership twice, but Dymond remained as president until January of 1969, when he resigned because of policy differences with its present owners, RKO General.

The second person, apparently, to hear of the sale was Richard Cooke of *The Wall Street Journal*. After the agreement had been reached orally, Baker flew to Los Angeles. On the following morning, he appeared at National's district sales office, which then was in the Biltmore Hotel, and for more than two hours he sat quietly on a divan doing nothing. About noon, Cooke called and asked to speak with him.

"Tell him I'm not here," Baker said.

Cooke was not so easily satisfied. "He says he knows you're here and he wants to talk to you about the sale of the airline," the startled secretary said presently.

"You tell him that if and when I sell the airline, I'll let him know," Baker replied, and then he laughed as the girl relayed the message.

Then, without another word, Baker left the office. He was back in Miami the next day. Why he came to Los Angeles and did nothing will probably forever remain a mystery.

Cooke, following the tradition of all good newsmen, will not tell where he got his tip that National had been sold.

The day Maytag walked into his new offices in Miami, one of his first suggestions was that the brown wrapping paper over the office windows be removed and be replaced with something more appropriate.

Maytag brought with him several key personnel from Frontier to National. These included G. Ray Woody, the executive vice president; J. Dan Brock, vice president of sales;

Edward J. Dolansky, vice president of finance; and William A. Nelson, vice president of legal affairs.

This transposition of personnel resulted in a humorous incident a few months later that Maytag delights in telling of. While riding to Los Angeles a few months later, he was reading a magazine relating to the aviation industry, and when he was finished, he placed it in the empty seat next to him. A man sitting across the aisle asked if he could see it, and, after skimming through it, he asked Maytag if he was connected with the aviation industry.

"Sort of," Maytag replied. "Are you?"

The man nodded. "I'm with Frontier."

"I've heard of them," Maytag said. "How are they doing?"

"Just great," the man replied. "Just great, since we got the new management."

It is Maytag's favorite story.

Immediately after Baker sold his National holdings, the market value of the stock went down steadily. The low point was approximately eleven dollars a share. Then slowly it began to rise. In California, Dudley Swim dumped all his holdings in Western Airlines and resigned from the airline's board of directors.

When National's stock reached fifteen dollars a share, Maytag sold one hundred thousand shares to Swim for approximately eighteen dollars a share, which, when translated to Maytag's investment, meant that he had paid $30.66 per share for the remaining hundred fifty thousand shares.

Baker became furious. Although he had agreed to Maytag's selling off one block of stock within sixty days without exercising his rights of first refusal, Baker apparently could only see the three quarters of a million dollars he would have made had he been given the opportunity to buy back the hundred thousand shares at the same price paid for them by Swim.

There were stories circulating around Miami that Baker had been jubilant over the sale originally, because he believed he had "taken" the young man from Denver. This feeling of jubilation turned into one of frustration when the market value of the stock steadily began to rise and, within less than six months, had gone through the price Maytag had paid for it. There were indications also that Baker had thought he was going to play a more dominant role in the operation of the airline than the one that was allocated to him.

The first indication to Maytag, however, that Baker was unhappy, came when he read in a newspaper that Baker had charged him with being incapable of running the airline and that he (Baker) probably would have to buy it back. The public charge was the first in a series of many. "I was a little upset," Maytag says wryly, "but I resisted the temptation to continue the fight by throwing press releases back at him." He went ahead with his plans to refinance the carrier and to get rid of its piston equipment, which was rapidly becoming obsolete.

Baker then filed suit against Maytag, claiming that their sales agreement had been breached when Maytag sold Swim the hundred thousand shares of stock without giving Baker the rights of first refusal. Baker also contended that another condition of the sale had been violated. The agreement called for each of the officers who was replaced to be given six months' notice. Those executives who were replaced and were given six months' salary in lieu of notice had been discharged in violation of the agreement, Baker claimed.

"Those who were relieved could have remained and drawn their salaries in twelve consecutive payments," Maytag says, "but men of executive caliber do not like to spend their time sitting behind a desk doing nothing."

It was Baker's contention that the six months' salary check paid in a lump sum did not constitute notice, and he claimed this as another contract violation.

Some time after the suit was filed, Maytag went to see Baker, who still maintained offices in the building that had housed Channel 10 when National owned it. "Ted Baker was chairman of the board," Maytag recalls. "I did not go to see him about the suit. It was my thought that Dudley Swim should be chairman of the board because of his big interest in the airline. I asked Ted if he had any objections to this."

"Why does he want to be chairman?" Baker asked.

"I'm not sure that he does. I am going to ask him to be chairman."

Baker nodded. "All right; it's okay with me."

Three weeks later there was a meeting of the board in the general offices of the airline. After most of the directors were in the board room, Baker arrived and indicated to Maytag that he wished to speak to him privately before the meeting started. The two men went into an empty adjacent office, and Baker handed Maytag a sheet of paper. It allegedly was the middle page of one of the many attachments to the brief sales contract. This attachment was a document that was, in effect, a consultant contract under which National had agreed to pay Baker thirty thousand dollars annually as an advisor. One clause in the contract said that Maytag would use his "best efforts" to assure that Baker had a seat on the board. The paper that Baker handed Maytag had the phrase "chairman of the board" rather than "seat on the board."

"According to our contract," Baker said, "I'm to be chairman of the board, and I'm not going to step down."

The board meeting was scheduled to start. Maytag's copy of the consultant contract was in the offices of John Love, his attorney, in Colorado. It would take at least a day to get his copy to Miami. Maytag shrugged and left the room. A few minutes later, he was closeted with Dudley Swim.

"I don't have my papers here. We can't try this case now, so let's don't even bring it up."

Swim chuckled softly over the unexpected development. "Okay," he said. "We won't even bring it up."

Two days after the meeting, Baker appeared unexpectedly in Maytag's office at National and dropped a paper on the desk. "I think you want this," he said.

Maytag picked it up. The paper was a written resignation by Baker of his chairmanship. The meeting was brief, but unusually harmonious for two men who were adversaries in a lawsuit. Baker commented that he was planning a trip to Europe sometime in the near future, and he inquired as to the health of Maytag's family. When he left, he paused in the doorway and looked around the office. Then, nodding once again, he went out. Maytag felt a distinct impression that it was at this moment that Baker psychologically sold the airline.

This impression in all probability is reality. Baker had no one left to fight, and to Baker a scrap was a necessary adjunct to life. He tried to fight Maytag, but Maytag would not even play the role of an elusive opponent. Baker thrived on discord and bustle. To Maytag, as stated previously, a great deal of movement does not mean a great deal of action.

There is an interesting incident that occurred at a meeting of the airline's executive committee shortly after Maytag assumed control, that points up the great differences between the two men. The executive committee at that time consisted of Maytag, Swim, Baker, Woody, and Truex, and it was meeting to consider a $51-million refinancing program that had been put together by Truex. Bob Truex had worked on it for several weeks. With seven banks participating, it covered all of National's indebtedness except an outstanding 10,288,000 issue of convertible subordinated debentures. Baker suddenly launched a virulent attack upon the whole program, which all the other members of the committee thought to be an excellent one. Truex was amazed, because as an expert in the banking business, he knew the program was extremely advantageous to National. Then, in the middle of his tirade, Baker looked across the table at Truex and winked.

When Baker was through, Maytag nodded politely, thanked him for his comments, then asked if anyone agreed. When no one did, Maytag nodded again. "Well, that's settled," he said quietly and turned to the next item on the agenda.

Maytag will make a suggestion quietly and presume, quite

correctly, that his suggestion will be carried out unless some valid reason is presented as to why it should not. Baker was more comfortable in the "belly to belly" argument, and if the argument carried over the entire office, he did not care.

During the Baker regime, the airline operated an executive dining room on the top floor. All of the company officers who were available were expected to attend the daily luncheons, which were called the "noon bloodletting."

Lew Dymond described these luncheons. "I can remember going up there and looking at a nice, rare steak. Baker would take off, and before I knew it, I was eating my dessert and had not touched my steak. He went through it every day with someone, and as a result one was exposed not only to his own problems but to those of every other department. Although all of us disliked them, I think they were beneficial."

There are others who disagree with Dymond. "I found it much more beneficial to have a quiet lunch with Maytag than a bloodletting with Baker," a former National officer says. "If Ted Baker didn't have someone to fight with over lunch, it was his lunch that was indeed miserable."

Bud Maytag would not fight with Ted Baker. Neither would Ray Woody, nor Dudley Swim, nor Bob Truex. They were soft-spoken men who did not subscribe to the theory that a bloodletting or a purge is conducive to efficiency.

It is quite possible that Baker finally realized this when he appeared at the board meeting with the puzzling second page of his consultant's contract. When he presented it to Maytag, it should have prompted a roar of rage. Instead Maytag replied with a shrug. The matter was not even discussed at the board meeting. It was then that he probably realized that Ted Baker and National Airlines no longer were synonymous.

A few months later, Ted, accompanied by his wife, left for a leisurely trip through Europe. One morning, he arose early, wrote a postcard to Lou Bower, mailed it, then walked toward a café for breakfast. As he entered the restaurant, he suffered another heart attack, and this time the seizure was fatal. His body was cremated in Europe. Memorial services were held in Miami, and the ashes were buried in the family plot at Pullman, Michigan, near the lake where he had played as a small boy.

CHAPTER THIRTEEN

Early in April of 1962, a few weeks before Maytag acquired control of National, King Taylor, the senior station manager in Los Angeles, reached the conclusion that the old air-conditioning truck used to cool the planes while they were on the ground would not last another season.

Taylor had been another of the group that had started with National in Jacksonville, and his tenure of service exceeded two decades. He had learned that the general office consisted of one person, Ted Baker. He knew also that all expenditures over five hundred dollars had to be scrutinized personally by Baker, and he had learned how Baker thought.

With this in mind, he planned his strategy according to Baker's line of reasoning. An air-conditioning truck did not have far to travel—just between the planes and the ramp—and thus a new truck was not really necessary. He scouted around the secondhand truck dealers in nearby Inglewood and Culver City, found one large enough to hold the air-conditioning unit on its bed, and cautiously gave the dealer a small deposit to hold the vehicle for a month.

He next checked over the air-conditioning unit and found that about 50% of it could be salvaged to the point where it could be used for another year. A few days later, he found a secondhand engine that would power it and some secondhand parts that would replace the worn-out portions.

He next wrote a long "authority for expenditure" request,

explaining that during the fall the temperatures at the Los Angeles Airport sometimes approached the 100° mark and that air conditioning for the parked planes was mandatory. He pointed out that a new unit cost around fifty thousand dollars, but that he had been able to put together a satisfactory substitute that should last at least a couple of years for under five thousand dollars.

Taylor's first thought, when he heard that the airline had been sold, was that the air-conditioning problem would remain unsolved for a long time and that he had lost his deposit on the truck. In one respect he was right. He did lose his deposit on his truck, and for several weeks he heard nothing on his AFE request. Then, in the first part of May, the AFE came back approved. It was approved, but someone had rewritten it so that it would authorize the purchase of a brand-new unit.

King Taylor's freshly lit cigar dropped out of his mouth. For a long time, he stared at the form. In his more than twenty years of service, he had never been authorized to buy a new piece of ground equipment when he could put together a secondhand substitute. "It was at this point I realized that the airline had really changed," he says.

The change was dramatic and immediate. In Miami, Maytag asked why National was known as the "Airline of the Stars." No one seemed to know. Someone suggested that the slogan had been substituted for an earlier one that had identified National as the "Route of the Buccaneers" and that this slogan had been abandoned when Rickenbacker had suggested publicly that it was most appropriate for a carrier run by an old pirate.

"If it has no meaning, let's get rid of it," Maytag suggested.

(The slogan actually was introduced as a sales promotion for status-conscious New Yorkers flying to Miami, implying that prominent Broadway and Hollywood actors flew on National exclusively.)

The planes were given a new paint job, and the old star

on the rudder was replaced with a modernistic "N." Within sixty days, Maytag, Woody, and Brock, traveling separately, had visited every city on the system, meeting employees and surveying the operation.

The "new look" was carried out on a wide front. The $51-million refinancing program consolidated the debt structure of the airline and enabled Maytag to dispose of all the piston equipment. Rather than wait a year for the delivery of new jets, Maytag picked up four Lockheed Electras from American Airlines and four long-range DC-8s from Northwest Orient to replace the void left by the loss of the piston propeller planes.

Two DC-7s were kept in service, but only because of the interchange agreement with Panagra. When the interchange agreement was drawn up, both Panagra and Pan Am were concerned about the quality of equipment that was to be used. At the time, the DC-7 was the best air transport flying, and the agreement called for the use of DC-7 equipment. It was intended to prevent Baker from using DC-6 or Constellation equipment on his part of the interchange, but after a few years it resulted in prohibiting National from using more advanced aircraft over the route.

There was another unforeseen development in the disposition of the piston planes. Most of them were sold in one transaction to Frederick B. Ayer & Associates Inc., a large aircraft broker headquartered in New York. At the time, Northeast was near the point of collapse. It was required to pay cash for its fuel, and at one station was even picking up National's dining service to cater its flights. A preponderance of its flight equipment was made up of British Vickers Viscounts, and about the time National disposed of its piston planes, Vickers repossessed the Viscounts it had sold to Northeast.

Ayer & Associates came to Northeast's rescue. They leased to Northeast the planes they had purchased from National, and thus, in effect, National was responsible for the continued existence of its struggling competitor.

Within a comparatively few weeks, National became a well-oiled, smoothly functioning machine. Its profits began to soar, and correspondingly so did the market value of the stock. The general opinion of the public was that the new management of the battle-scarred carrier was responsible, but Maytag says this is not true. With the acquisition of the Southern Trans-continental Route, there was no way but up. "It would have gone up with Baker, but possibly not as rapidly, because we had better financing behind us than he did."

Truex describes it this way: "National's financing situation (under Baker) was not necessarily any worse than any of the other trunk lines. During its dark days it took the best kind of a credit deal it could find, and some of these came under pretty stringent terms."

An example is the fact that National was the largest stock-holder in Pan American, holding about 6% of the stock. This stock was pledged to secure a $4.5-million loan. "It just wasn't the right type of a loan," Truex says. "National was in a situation where it had several loans that should have been folded into one and at the same time raise enough money for the purchase of new equipment."

Under the refinancing program, seven banks were brought in. Traditionally, Chemical Bank and Trust of New York had been the lead bank in loans to National, and it was the opinion of the new board of directors that they should continue to be a participant because they had seen the airline through some very dark days. Other participating banks were the First National City Bank of New York, the First National Bank of Miami, Bank of the Southwest in Houston, United California Bank in Los Angeles, Bank of America in San Francisco, and, of course, the Irving Trust.

"This was not altogether because the new management was a collective genius," Truex says. "It was because the times were changing. The airline business was in for an upward swing in the cycle. I don't have any reason in the world to think that Baker couldn't have done it."

Other National executives agree, although one of the older executives has a qualification. "Sure, Baker could have done it, but the odds are good that he would not have."

Early in 1961, National had sold, through Lehman Brothers, approximately $10 million of convertible debentures. One of the first steps undertaken by the new management was an attempt to call in these debentures, as they represented a dilution of about one third of the outstanding shares. The market of the stock was such that the board thought that probably 95% of the debentures would have been turned in for cash. The attempt to raise the extra $10 million was unsuccessful, although there was one offer from a large insurance corporation that was rejected by the board. Today, almost all of the debenture issue has been converted.

Under the Maytag regime, the airline retains about half of its net worth in cash flow every year in profit plus depreciation. This is where most of the money comes from to pay for new equipment. The rest of it is borrowed from the syndicate of seven banks. National today is the only trunk carrier in the United States that does not have any long-term debts. It owes no money to the insurance companies nor to the public, and every other trunk carrier in the United States does.

There was another problem facing the airline. It owned four hundred thousand shares of Pan American stock, and Pan Am owned a similar amount of National stock, the result of the leasing agreement entered into by the two carriers in 1958. The Civil Aeronautics Board had ordered both carriers to divest themselves of each other's stock. Nothing had been done about it, however, partially because Baker had pledged National's shares in Pan Am as security for a loan. Also, there was a discrepancy in the comparative market value of the stock.

Under the refinancing program, this stock was released as a security. Maytag immediately started negotiations with

Trippe to exchange the stock, but Trippe was reluctant to do so. The negotiations dragged on for several weeks with no progress. Maytag finally decided he would sell National's Pan Am holdings on the open market.

A "no-action" letter was obtained from the Securities and Exchange Commission, which meant in effect that National was free to sell the stock without a registration. It meant also that the unloading of so many shares of Pan Am stock on the market surely would depress the share value.

Arrangements to sell the stock were made with a prominent New York brokerage firm. The night before the sale, the treasurer of Pan American, Robert G. Ferguson, called Bob Truex and said mildly that Pan Am really did not want the stock to go on sale.

"We don't really want to sell it," Truex replied.

"Why don't we swap it back?"

"Okay, let's swap it back," Truex agreed, and told Ferguson to call Ed Dolansky and get his advice on the particulars.

The stock was exchanged on a share-for-share basis.

There remained only one other financial headache—the suit filed against Maytag by Baker. Mrs. Baker continued with it after her husband's death "just as a matter of business." She lost in the lower court and appealed, but the appeal was denied. She appealed again and lost in the higher court. The final decision was issued late in 1968.

During the litigation, however, she expressed a considerable respect for Maytag, which was reciprocated. At a luncheon in Miami Springs in 1964, which was celebrating National's 30th birthday, Irma Baker, her daughter Barbara, and Maytag shared the head table.

Mrs. Baker has since remarried and divides her time between North Carolina and Miami.

PART TWO

Pilots are inclined to refer to aircraft as birds, and these birds play a most important part in the structure of an airline if for no other reason than that, without them, there would be no airline. The type of equipment purchased by carriers has made airlines and it has broken carriers.

There are many who believe that Capitol Airlines collapsed because its fleet consisted of Vickers Viscounts, a British-made turboprop that was one of the first to be manufactured. It was a fast and comfortable aircraft with large windows, and it won immediate public acceptance, yet its range was limited, and this made it an impractical aircraft for use by United States carriers. There is a story often told, a story that may be apocryphal, that if Capitol suffered more than a twenty-minute air traffic control delay on one of its longer-haul routes out of New York, the pilot had to return to the ramp for refueling.

When Boeing converted the B-29 bomber of World War II into a plush, double-decker Stratocruiser, it was hailed as the epitome of luxury in air transport. Few airlines bought them, however, as the cost of operation was so great that they required 10% more passengers than the aircraft could hold for the airline to break even financially on a flight of medium distance.

Today, with all airlines operating under the corporate and computer syndrome, it is extremely unlikely that any manufacturer ever will be able to sell a plane like a Stratocruiser to a carrier. Increased speed no longer is a criterion in the subsonic jet era, because all jet transports cruise at about the same rate of speed. A DC-8 on an experimental non-stop flight from Tokyo to Miami actually broke the sound barrier, so proving to the Federal Aviation Authority that there was actually no safety barrier and that a pending ruling limiting the speed of jets was pointless. The Boeing 727 has cruised for hours just under Mach 1, which is the speed of sound.

Until Maytag acquired control of National, its fleet had been acquired more upon the availability of equipment than the purchase of aircraft best tailored to the needs of its route structure. The airline was born as a result of the two Ryans. It came into being, not because the Ryans were the best equipment for the route, but because Baker had two Ryans he wished to utilize. The Stinsons that replaced these two aircraft were acquired because they were surplus to Western Airlines and were available at a price Baker could afford to pay.

The durability of these Stinsons is attested to by the fact that one of them is reported to be still flying in Alaska today. Baker sold it early in 1940 to a "big bush pilot with a red beard" who lifted up his shirt, pulled out eighteen hundred dollars from a money belt to pay for it, then flew it away.

The first new aircraft to be purchased by National were the original Lockheed Electras, and these were followed by two Lockheed Lodestars. The Lodestars were cheaper and smaller than the DC-2s and DC-3s used by National's biggest competitor. They were more difficult to enter and to move around inside because of a huge spar in the center of the fuselage, although the spar often delighted male passengers, as it forced a considerable hoisting of the skirts of stewardesses while moving from one end of the cabin to the other. The DC-3 carried twenty-one passengers; the Lodestar carried fourteen. The Lodestar, however, was much faster, and to Baker the speed far outweighed the other disadvantages of the Lockheed. On November 2, 1940, he set a new southern transcontinental record in a Lodestar when he flew one from Los Angeles to Jacksonville in nine hours and twenty-nine minutes.

For a while, the public demand for speed proved the wisdom of Baker's choice. On National's routes that were competitive with Eastern, a good load was a dozen passengers, and Baker's dozen was assured by the fact that he could depart later than Eastern and arrive earlier. The pilots, according to instructions, would always point out an Eastern flight when it was overtaken in the air, and if Baker was on a flight when this happened, the stewardess knew he would be in a fine humor for the remainder of the trip.

Baker's competitive advantage of speed, however, fell apart with the start of World War II. Under the priority system allocated by the federal government to travelers, every seat on every flight was full, and the difference of the seven additional seats on the DC-3 over the Lodestar cost National many, many thousands of dollars in revenue.

The losses were recouped at the end of the war. The global conflict had made it obvious that the twin-engine piston plane was obsolescent, practical only on short-haul routes. Eastern apparently decided early in the war that it would re-equip its fleet with four-engine Lockheed Constellations. Baker decided also in favor of the Constellations, but his decision came too late. All the early delivery positions had been taken by Eastern and TWA, and Baker suddenly found himself in the position of running his midget Lockheed Lodestars in competition with Eastern's giant Connies. The Lodestars were short range, and were required to hop, skip, and jump up and down the East Coast on the lucrative New York–Miami run. The Constellations could carry almost as many passengers as five Lodestars and, additionally, could make the trip nonstop. When Baker realized what had happened, he appealed desperately to TWA for help, offering a "fantastic premium" for two of their early delivery positions for the Constellation, but TWA, which also was in a competitive situation, was uninterested.

He went to Los Angeles and conferred with officials of the Douglas Aircraft Corporation, but the situation was little better there. Douglas was planning to convert the C-54, a four-engine military transport, into a commercial aircraft, but here again delivery positions were far down the line. More than a year would pass before he could put a four-engine transport across from Eastern on the East Coast routes.

While Baker was in Santa Monica, however, he was given a tour of the plant by Douglas brass that included an inspection of the military C-54s under construction for the Army Air Corps. It was well known that the end of the war was imminent, and Baker asked the obvious question: "If the war ended tomorrow, what would happen to these?"

It was explained to him that production of the military version probably would cease immediately and that Douglas would be paid under the cost-plus procedures only for the amount of construction that had been completed. Baker learned also that they could be modified into a civilian version and that none of these partially constructed aircraft were designated for delivery positions for other airlines when the war ended. Nor were there any legal barriers involving disposition of the aircraft. Before Baker left California he signed a provisional contract to purchase four of the C-54s, to be converted to DC-4s in conformance with National's specifications.

Baker had little more than a month to wait before the Japanese capitulated. Some two to three weeks later, he purchased a war-weary C-54 that had been declared surplus by the Air Corps and secretly started the transitional pilot training from the Lodestars to the four-engine equipment. National took delivery from Douglas on its first DC-4 on February 12, 1946, and two days later, on Valentine's Day, inaugurated non-stop service between New York and Miami. When service was authorized into Havana the same year, the DC-4s were also placed on this run, and by the time the fourth DC-4 was delivered, these aircraft were in service all over National's route structure. The competitive advantage over Eastern was almost monopolistic, as the latter carrier still was flying the slower, short-range DC-3s. In order to regain its share of the market, Eastern purchased some war-surplus DC-4s from the military and converted them to civilian use, but it was almost a year before they were put in service. Thus, for almost a year, National's load factors soared, and for no other reason than its utilization of more comfortable and faster equipment in its fleet. It was an advantage that was to reverse itself in the not-too-distant future.

At the end of World War II, all the airlines in the United States were competitive, as they are now, and the competitive advantages went to the carrier with the best equipment.

The percentage of the population within the United States that traveled by air was very low. There were few monopoly routes, and not only National and Eastern, but all the airlines, spent more time and effort fighting each other for this existing business than they did in promoting the advantages of air travel to the more than 95% of the population that never flew.

Because of this competition, the airlines demanded faster and larger aircraft with greater range. The manufacturers were delighted to oblige, and so was launched a re-equipment cycle that was to plague the carriers for more than a decade. New models, or improved versions of existing models, appeared almost every year. Speed was the criterion, and more speed meant higher costs of operation and higher initial costs for equipment. To compensate for this, the newer aircraft had to be made larger in order to carry more passengers.

Two years after the war, an airline flying a DC-6 between New York and Los Angeles could make the round trip with fifty passengers on board in about the same length of time it would take a DC-3 to travel one leg of the trip with only twenty-one passengers. This comparison is known in the airline industry as seat-mile capacity—the number of seats that can be moved in a given time at a given cost over a given distance. The load factor is the number of people carried on board an airplane on a given flight, and the break-even load factor is the percentage of the seats that must be sold on a given flight to pay for the costs of the flight. Thus, with twice the capacity, twice the speed, and twice the range, National's load factors soared, and, correspondingly, so did its profits in this period of nearly a year when Baker held his equipment advantage over Rickenbacker.

Between 1945 and 1953, the Douglas Aircraft Corporation introduced six different versions of a four-engine piston transport, ranging from the DC-4 to the DC-7C. Lockheed remodeled its Constellation eight times during the same period.

The first commercial transport offered by Douglas after the DC-4 was the DC-6. (The DC-5 was an experimental version never offered for sale.) National ordered the DC-6 and took delivery on the first of these aircraft on July 1, 1947. With these planes, the flying time from New York to Miami was cut from five hours to four hours, and National, for a time, was still able to maintain its competitive advantage over Eastern, which was taking delivery of its Constellations. The DC-6, however, had a mechanical flaw that caused a series of crashes on other airlines. When this plane was introduced, there still was a regulation from the CAA in effect that required all commercial aircraft to carry magnesium flares under the wings.

In the days of the Ryans and the Stinsons, this regulation made some sense, because it allowed the pilot of a crippled aircraft to drop his flare at night and possibly locate a pasture or an open field in which he could make a forced landing. With the DC-4s and 6s, however, such rules were obsolete, as there were no pastures smooth enough or large enough to accommodate such an emergency landing.

The DC-6As were catching fire in the air, and when the flames reached these flares, the magnesium burned with such intensity that the plane was destroyed in flight. After a few such crashes, the regulation was rescinded.

In November of 1948, an American Airlines DC-6 traveling from Los Angeles to New York caught fire in midair, but the pilot was able to land the aircraft on a small airport in Gallup, New Mexico, and the blaze was quickly extinguished by means of waiting fire trucks. A subsequent investigation disclosed that some of the fuel gauges on the flight deck were faulty. Gasoline was fed to the engines from the inboard tanks on the wings, and when the gauges would show these inner tanks were low, the pilot would pump gas from the outer tanks into the inner tanks. Because of the faulty gauges, the pumping would continue after the inner tanks were full. The excess fuel then would drain through an overflow valve, cling to the body of the plane, and then enter a small scoop connected to the aircraft's heating system, where it would ignite.

As soon as the cause of the fires was established, all the DC-6s were grounded until proper modifications could be made to the aircraft. This grounding suddenly reversed the competitive advantage National had held over Eastern. It took three months to modify the aircraft, and, during this peak tourist season, National, flying its slower DC-4s, gave up most of the market to Eastern, with its fleet of Constellations. The flying public wanted speed, and Eastern was faster.

The DC-7 was a major modification of the DC-6, and there are some at Douglas who say it was built only on the insistence of C. R. Smith, president of American Airlines, who wanted a faster piston plane and one that could fly non-stop from New York to Los Angeles.

Baker bought the DC-7 because it was faster than Ricken-backer's Constellations. From an operational viewpoint, the plane was not good. Its powerful Wright engines were temperamental, and the operation costs far exceeded those of the DC-6. Baker himself piloted the first one to be delivered to National and flew it non-stop at maximum speed from Santa Monica to Miami. Again he set a new southern transcontinental speed record, but when he landed in Miami, it developed that his efforts had burned out three of the four engines on the aircraft. When told of this by Walter Sternberg, his vice president of sales and traffic, Baker laughed.

"What the hell," he replied. "They are still faster than anything Rickenbacker's got."

This was the thought—the idea of beating Rickenbacker—upon which Baker dwelt gleefully and constantly. For the short-haul routes he bought Convairs, the new twin-engine transport, to put across from Eastern's DC-3s.

The majority of the Lodestars were put up for sale, and a United States broker offered Baker eighty-five thousand dollars each for them, but before the contract was signed, Baker received another, more attractive offer from a newly formed Argentinian airline. The Lodestars were ferried to Buenos Aires. Baker never saw them again, nor did he ever receive any payment for them. The new airline ran into financial difficulties in its formation, and the planes were all attached to satisfy the creditors. Baker sued in the Argentine courts, and the Lodestars were set aside on a small airport until the case could be settled. The case still hangs in the courts, and the Lodestars reportedly are still sitting on the airport almost twenty years later.

Baker bought four Lockheed Constellations to run on night coach flights between Miami and New York, and for all this varied equipment he had to stock hundreds of thousands of dollars' worth of spare parts in the various system cities of the carrier.

A long time later, these Constellations were converted to freighters, but National and very few other airlines have been able to operate an air freighter profitably, despite the continuing glowing predictions about the future of air freight. The trunk lines are carrying a considerable volume in air freight both in jet freighters and in the bellies of jet passenger aircraft, but it is still a "break-even" business under the best of circumstances.

Early in the fifties, Baker decided that a helicopter service would prove a profitable adjunct to the system, and he applied for permission to provide scheduled helicopter service within a hundred-fifty-mile radius of Miami International Airport, and a short time later, an extensive route in Virginia. The request was approved, and on February 1, 1954, service was inaugurated in Miami with a Sikorsky S-55. The helicopter route extended from the Florida Keys to West Palm Beach with schedules to a number of municipalities as well as the race tracks at Hialeah, Tropical Park, and Gulfstream.

On the inaugural flight to West Palm Beach, the first person off the helicopter was John L. Morris; the first person to greet him was a West Palm Beach cop, who handed him a ticket for illegally parking a helicopter. In Miami Beach, the city fathers became so irate over the noise of the chopper that they tore up the city heliport and thus solved their noise-abatement problem. National learned early what many other helicopter-line operators discovered later—that there was no profit in running a chopper. The machine was sold, and the routes around Virginia never were activated.

With Baker's lust for battle against Eastern, it is strange that he would allow himself to be outmaneuvered by Rickenbacker in the late fifties in almost the same manner as had occurred toward the end of World War II.

About two years after the first DC-7 was flown away from the Douglas Airport in Santa Monica, the Lockheed Company came out with the turboprop Electra, a propeller-driven transport powered by four jet engines and carrying ninety persons. The delivery price was about three million dollars.

With the arrival of the Electra, many airline executives thought the equipment race had reached a plateau. Cruising at four hundred fifty miles per hour, this turboprop transport had reached the maximum speed physically allowable for propeller-driven planes with a straight wing. The pure jet transport was believed to be at least ten years in the future, an attitude that was fed in detail by the tragic experiences of the British with their first jetliner, the Comet. Baker was offered some early delivery positions on the Electra line by Lockheed, but he vacillated, hoping his delay would cause Lockheed to come down on the unit price. Lockheed, however, was in a position of strength, and while the bargain-conscious Baker waited patiently for Lockheed to meet his terms, the airframe manufacturer sold its first sixty-two delivery positions to American, Eastern, and Western. In the summer of 1958, Baker apparently realized for the first time that Eastern would be operating Electras against National's slower piston equipment during the heavy winter tourist season.

There are some at National who believe Baker's delay in ordering Electras was prompted by the knowledge that the pure-jet transports were much closer than most persons in the airline industry realized and that he had hoped to make the jump from piston to pure jet, bypassing the transitional turboprop. It is possible, but unlikely, because of Baker's penchant for making a deal. It was a "deal" that turned National toward the Douglas DC-8 jets rather than the Boeing 720s that Baker preferred, and it was still another "deal" that bailed Baker out of his difficulties in competing with Eastern during the 1958 winter tourist season.

Pure jets were much closer in the fifties than most persons realized. The Boeing Company, which had long lagged behind Douglas and Lockheed in sales of commercial transports, had been building a jet air tanker for the military. This military air tanker was known as the K-135, and it was the prototype for the now famous Boeing 707 transport. The first 707s were delivered to Pan American in 1958. A shorter-range version of this aircraft, and somewhat smaller, was the Boeing 720.

During the summer of 1958, while both Boeing and Douglas were trying to sell their jet transports to National, Baker went to New York to meet with Juan Trippe and to discuss a proposition. In view of his previous experience with Baker, it is incredible that Trippe would entertain any kind of business proposition from Baker, but the proposal superficially was a good one for both National and Pan American.

Baker suggested that National lease two of Pan American's jets during the peak winter months of 1958 and 1959, which was Pan Am's lowest traffic period. For an added incentive, Baker offered to exchange four hundred thousand shares of National stock for an equal amount of Pan Am stock on a one-for-one basis. Additionally, however, Pan American would be given an option on an additional two hundred fifty thousand shares, which was enough to give Pan American control of National. The prospect of linking his Miami and New York gateways, as well as access to the New York–Miami market, was too much for Juan Trippe to resist.

In the latter part of August, Baker returned to Miami and conferred with Lew Dymond. The deal for the lease of the Pan American jets was made, but National had no one on its payroll who was capable of flying them. Not only did the airline have less than three months to check out its pilots and flight engineers, but it also had to work out an agreement between the Flight Engineers Union and ALPA. The jets were so new, there really was nothing to use as a criterion for agreements. No airline had any such agreement, including Pan Am, which was flying its planes with supervisory pilots. No one, including Baker, thought all the details could be worked out before the Miami "season" started.

Nevertheless, flight crews were sent to New York for transition training in Pan Am's jets. The crews trained while Lew Dymond and Jerry Rosenthal, National's vice president of industrial relations, worked with representatives of the union.

Meanwhile, Eastern had launched a heavy advertising program promoting the Electras as the quickest way to reach Miami during the 1958–59 winter season. Baker waited with the patience of a veteran showman to make his announcement. Then, in little more than a week before he was to put the leased Pan American jets into service, he made his announcement of the new jet service by full-page ads in both the Miami and New York newspapers. The inauguration of service was started on December 10, 1958, and on board the first south-bound flight were such celebrities as Ronald Coleman, Gypsy Rose Lee, and Bob Considine.

Baker also arranged to have forty seats sold to the manage-ment of the Hialeah racetrack, who passed them out to some of the heavier players in New York. Tom Shea, who also was on the flight, remembers that it was "thirteen degrees cold in New York when we boarded and eighty-five degrees warm when we landed."

A reporter interviewed Gypsy Rose Lee upon her arrival in Miami and asked for an opinion of her first ride in a jet transport. "It's the first plane I have ever seen that actually has a john that flushes," the candid Miss Lee replied.

More remarkable was the fact that an agreement had so quickly been reached with the unions, and it was an agreement that today has proved the norm for the industry.

Baker shuttled the two leased 707s around the clock be-tween New York and Miami, and there were few flights on which the load factor was not 100%. In many cases, travelers postponed their departures in order to take advantage of trav-eling by jet, and all this was at the expense of a frustrated Eastern and the still struggling Northeast Airlines, who di-vided the leftover traffic between them.

The cost of leasing the jets was the normal operating ex-pense plus minor profit for Pan American. The appeal to Pan American in the deal, however, was the stock options, and transactions such as these required the blessing of the Civil Aeronautics Board. The CAB, like all governmental agencies, moves slowly and ponderously, and their considera-tion of the transaction dragged on through the entire winter season, every day of which National was reaping huge profits with Pan American's jets.

In the spring, when the heavy Florida season was over, the CAB disapproved of the entire transaction. Baker apologetically returned the Pan American jets to a furious Juan Trippe. Baker had no further need for them. His three medium-range DC-8s were scheduled for delivery well before the next season.

Later on, he had some anxious moments. The Douglas Corporation fell behind in their production schedule, and there were a few weeks in the early summer when it appeared possible that Baker would not have his planes in time for training crews before the heavy tourist season. For some reason, he blamed Jackson McGowan, one of the Douglas executives, for his trouble.

One warm summer day, Baker appeared at a gate of the Douglas plant in Long Beach and told the guard that he wanted to see McGowan.

"What is your name, sir?"

"Baker."

The guard picked up the telephone and called McGowan's secretary. "There's a Mr. Baker to see Mr. McGowan."

The secretary was efficient. "Would you ask him what he wants?" she asked crisply.

The guard relayed the message.

"Just tell him I want my goddam airplanes," Baker roared. Only then did anyone at Douglas realize that the Baker waiting at the gate was the president of National Airlines.

Baker did get his jets in time. The day the first one was delivered, Donald Douglas, Jr., presented Baker with an expensive shotgun as a tangible apology for the delay. "There's just one condition to this gift," he said as he gave the gun to Baker. "Don't use it to shoot Jackson McGowan."

The arrival of the pure jets was not an immediate financial bonanza for the nation's carriers. Shortly after Maytag assumed control of National, he referred to the years of 1960 and 1961 as the era of "jet indigestion" for the airlines. All the airlines rushed to buy jets. The unit cost plus the required spare parts was about three times higher than the most expensive propeller equipment. The old formula, which had been the rule for almost twenty years, that more speed and more seats in an airplane meant greater profits was not holding up.

The cost of a pure-jet transport was about six million dollars. It carried approximately one hundred fifty persons and cruised at about six hundred miles per hour, thus traveling across the continent in approximately five hours. To move the same number of persons from one coast to the other would take two weeks in one DC-3. One Electra would require twenty-four hours to accomplish the same movement.

The airlines rushed to the manufacturers, buying from whichever company could first promise delivery. By late 1960, most of the nation's trunk carriers were jet equipped, and as more and more subsonic jets went into service, the airlines slowly began to realize that their seat-mile capacity exceeded the demand.

A seat in an airplane is a commodity to be sold, but it obviously can be sold only as a moving object. Enough persons, in theory, must rent, or buy, a seat with sufficient frequency to keep the plane in the air enough hours to pay for the operating costs, the overhead, and the capital investment, and to provide the stockholders of the company a profit.

Early in 1961, the three trunk carriers operating between New York and Los Angeles were offering a total of eighteen hundred seats daily between the two cities. But the number of persons buying seats on these flights was much less than the offering. The same situation developed along the eastern seaboard. Northeast and Eastern were running jets in competition with National, and all three carriers beagn to operate at a loss. In 1960 National's losses were $2.9 million and the following year were a huge $7.25 million despite its inauguration of service in early June to the West Coast along the Southern Transcontinental Route.

During this era of jet indigestion, the airlines had gone millions of dollars into debt to purchase the new equipment and necessary spare parts, and their monthly losses reached staggering proportions. Some carriers could not afford the transition and collapsed. Others developed such poor financial condition that Alan Boyd, then chairman of the Civil Aeronautics Board, recommended merger of many of the carriers as the only alternative to collapse. Yet the subsonic jet transport, which almost ruined the industry, has proved its greatest boon. It is the safest, the most economical, and the most comfortable mode of air transportation ever known. Operating costs have reached such a low point that National can operate a non-stop flight between Los Angeles and Miami with a break-even load factor as low as 34%. The percentage of the American population using air travel has showed a steady upsurge, partially because the fear of flight died along with the older generation, and partially because of the acceptance of the fact that jet air transports are the most logical means by which to move from one point to another.

Along with the steady rise in air travel, the airlines found a residual benefit in the conversion to jets. The necessary re-equipment cycle, which had drained a large portion of their profits into the treasuries of the manufacturers, was broken. No longer were they forced to buy new planes every two years because of a slight increase in speed. The first 707 that came off the assembly line flies no faster than the 707 that will be finished tomorrow. There have been minor improvements over the years, but none of sufficient importance to warrant the trading in of one model upon another. One of the most publicized improvements a few years ago was the "fan-jet engine," but the improvement was only a saving in fuel consumption.

All subsonic jets fly just below the threshold of the speed of sound, or Mach 1, and a passenger can board a jet that has flown the equivalent of fifty round trips to the moon and reach his destination within the same elapsed time as if he boarded a jet on its maiden flight. Thus one of the basic factors that forced the airlines to buy new equipment every two or three years, speed, was removed when the manufacturers brought their transports up to the sound barrier. The other factor is the number of seats that can be placed in an aircraft, and this has resulted in a curious situation in the industry.

One of Maytag's first acts when he took over National was to clean up the fleet, which was a hodgepodge of various types of equipment. All the obsolete piston equipment was sold. A refinancing program wiped out the leasing agreements for DC-8s with Douglas, leaving nine owned by National. A short time later, four secondhand DC-8s were purchased from Northwest Orient Airlines, for a total of thirteen. Four secondhand Electras were purchased from American Airlines, bringing up to seventeen the number of prop-jets in the fleet. About the same time, negotiations were carried out for the purchase of thirteen Boeing 727s. It was Maytag's intention to retire the Electras coincidentally with the delivery of the Boeing 727s.

During this first half of the sixties, however, the demand for available seats increased much more rapidly than anticipated by most persons in the airline and airframe-manufacturing industries. The airlines, including National, wanted more seats, but because income had been eroded rather heavily by "gimmick" competitive fares, the airlines also wanted to save operational costs. The result was the birth of the "stretchout."

Douglas added thirty feet to the fuselage of its standard DC-8, thereby increasing the number of passengers it could carry by approximately fifty. The price of a standard DC-8 had gone up to about $8 million, and the price of a stretchout was about $10 million.

Each airline has a slightly different configuration of its equipment, but for the sake of comparison, it can be assumed that the standard DC-8 has a capacity of one hundred fifty passengers and the stretchout more than two hundred. Operational costs of a stretchout are about the same as a standard, but it requires three standards to carry about the same number of passengers as two stretchouts. Three standards cost about $24 million as against a $20-million price tag for two stretchouts. Thus, in addition, the airline saved the operational costs of another airplane.

Boeing was quick to copy Douglas, although the company could only stretch out its medium-range, three-engine 727. The 707, which had launched the jet era in the United States, was built so close to the ground that if the fuselage were extended the tail would hit the runway every time the pilot pulled back on the controls to take off. Boeing also designed the behemoth 747, which carries more than twice as many passengers as the DC-8 stretchout, costs twice as much, and is scheduled to be in service by 1970. National is flying twenty-five 727 stretchouts and two DC-8 stretchouts and has two 747s scheduled for delivery in 1970. With the delivery of the 727 stretchouts, the Electras were sold.

National has made no plans to purchase a supersonic transport. A few years ago, the acquisition of SSTs was expected to be the next major re-equipment cycle to face the airlines, and in the early 1960s one American trunk carrier was boasting that it would be flying a supersonic jet transport on its domestic routes before the end of 1966. Nevertheless, the SST debacle has had a residual effect upon National and the other trunk carriers in this country.

In 1963, Pan American Airways issued a press release announcing the order of fifteen Concorde SSTs, an aircraft built jointly by the British and the French and which is designed to fly at approximately fifteen hundred miles per hour and carry between one hundred and one hundred thirty passengers. At the time of the announcement, the Concorde had progressed beyond its theoretical stage, and little, if anything, had been done toward the development of a competitive aircraft within the United States.

Nevertheless, the Pan American announcement caused consternation in American governmental and aircraft-manufacturing circles. A few hours after the order was made public, the late President Kennedy departed from a prepared text of a speech he was delivering before the Air Force Academy in

Colorado Springs to announce that the United States would launch a crash program to construct a supersonic transport that would be bigger and faster and better than the British and French endeavor. The cost of constructing this American SST prototype would be in excess of one billion dollars. Of this initial cost, the government would put up 75%. The remaining $250 million in estimated development costs would come from the airframe manufacturer whose concept of the SST was deemed most practical by the government. The program would be administered by the Federal Aviation Authority.

The plan was received with loud huzzahs, and several airlines in the United States, including Pan American, rushed to the FAA with large deposits for the American version of an SST aircraft that was non-existent.

North American, which built the experimental supersonic RB-70, indicated interest in participating in the U.S. commercial supersonic program. So did Boeing and Lockheed. Conversely, Douglas, which for years had been a leader in commercial air-transport manufacture, wanted no part of the SST and refused to bid for it. The preliminary proposals of Boeing and Lockheed were accepted by the FAA, and these two manufacturers were authorized to proceed with the development of detailed airframe designs. The general impression given to the public was that the SST was imminent and that within two or three years New Yorkers would be whisked to Miami within a few minutes, to Los Angeles or San Francisco within a couple of hours. To disagree was blasphemy.

Yet Bud Maytag did disagree, and some of his predictions have proved uncannily accurate. In a speech before the National Aerospace Education Council in Miami Beach, Florida, a little more than a month after the Kennedy announcement, Maytag questioned several points in the proposal, suggesting that a Mach 3, American-built SST was at least fifteen years in the future, if not more.

The early conceptions of the aircraft were based on the retractable-wing theory, and Maytag publicly questioned the advisability of this because of the weight factor and other reasons. He suggested also that the development of a Mach 2 aircraft similar to the British-French Concorde not be so casually discarded.

"The majority of our airplane manufacturers have been supporting the development of a Mach 3 aircraft," he said. "Recently, the head of the supersonic study team for a manufacturer voiced the attitude of many people in the industry when he predicted that a Mach 2 transport faces the danger of premature obsolescence.

"Industry leaders in manufacturing decry the Mach 2 since aluminum loses strength through aerodynamic heating above Mach 2.4 or 1,500 miles per hour. They indicate that the growth of such a plane would be forever limited. A Mach 2 transport can be constructed of aluminum whereas the Mach 3 must have a basic structure of titanium and steel."

Maytag went on in his speech to urge that the manufacturers in the United States develop a Mach 2 aircraft, and warned that, if they did not, "American trunk carriers will be forced to turn to foreign manufacturers.

"I believe that if we concentrate in the United States upon the refinement of an economically efficient Mach 2 transport, we will continue to lead the world in the manufacture of commercial aircraft.

"On a Mach 2 aircraft of American manufacture, the development costs are not so great but that they can be absorbed by private industry. We will be competing on an even basis with the French and British consortium, but we will have a tremendous advantage because there will be rival ventures within the United States."

The speech attracted considerable criticism from many sources, but it is interesting to note the development of the SST since Maytag made his speech in 1963.

The Concorde prototype, a Mach 2 aircraft, is flying. So is

a similar Russian version. In the United States, both Lockheed and Boeing won government financing to proceed with the original design of a Mach 3 aircraft. In late 1966, the government chose the Boeing concept over the Lockheed design. The Boeing version was a highly sophisticated piece of machinery with retractable swing wings. The Lockheed concept was a less-complicated aircraft of double delta-wing design. After Boeing won the award, it ran into trouble with its design. One of the basic problems was the development of a movable wing that could be used practically on a commercial SST transport. The winning proposal was scrapped, and Boeing began redesigning its plane more along the lines of the winning Lockheed proposal.

The contention that the Mach 2 version would become obsolete too quickly has been disproved by the passage of time. The knowledgeable *Aviation Daily* has stated that the earliest the American SST can be certificated is in 1976. This is eighteen years after the certification of the first subsonic jet. In the eighteen years on the other side of 1958, the aircraft manufacturing industry evolved from the DC-3 transport to the jet transport.

It is unlikely that any American-built commercial SST will be flying for many years. As of mid-1969, no decision had been reached by the federal government as to whether the SST development program should proceed or be killed, although design experimentation still was being financed by funds previously appropriated by the government. The prototypes for the Concorde are flying, but design changes are needed, and there are numerous reports of disagreement between the French and British partners in the project. The latest target for a date in which a certificate of airworthiness will be issued is late in 1972. Most persons in the airline industry do not think the deadline will be met.

The controversy still continues in Washington. Recently Representative Fletcher Thompson, of Georgia, a member of the House Commerce Committee, suggested that the United

States scrap its plans to build a Mach 2.5 commercial SST and build a Mach 4 or 5 aircraft that will be available for sale to airlines in the late seventies.

About the same time, sources at both the Federal Aviation Authority and the Boeing Company stated that they have "literally given up" the idea of flying any true SST on regular, commercial, transcontinental routes because of the unsolvable problem of the sonic boom.

Then Lockheed announced a project it had been keeping a secret since the loss of its SST design proposal to Boeing. It disclosed that it had designed a Low Supersonic Transport (LST), a 450-passenger airplane that could fly 2,875 miles at Mach 1.15, up to 40% faster than the current subsonic jets. With this speed, at a cruising altitude of 44,000 feet, it would not cause any noticeable sonic boom. The engines used would be the same Pratt & Whitney JT9D model, with minor modifications, as is used on the jumbo Boeing 747s. With Lockheed's running start on such a project, its potential sales could reach as high as seven hundred.

"This may tend to increase," said *Aviation Daily*, "as aviation customers lose patience as the government continues to stall on (the SST) program go-ahead. Experience has proven initial designs usually can be pushed to attain greater range and while the LST today is configured for 2,800 miles, it conceivably could go to 3,500. Carriers who want to fly a U.S. product may begin to look with greater and greater favor on an airplane which might not meet the Russian TU-144 and the Anglo-French Concorde Mach number, but which would beat them on payload and, most important, be available before the U.S. SST."

Ray Woody also offered some comments of a critical nature on the SST, in a speech delivered in Cleveland. His speech also attracted wide attention in the industry, and one of the more interesting comments came from Dan Partner, the aviation editor of the Denver *Post*.

"Among recent disappointments was the failure of proponents of the U. S. Supersonic Transport (SST) to answer a criticism of the billion-dollar project by National Airlines executive G. Ray Woody," Partner wrote. "He left nothing to the imagination in lashing the venture in an address at Cleveland, Ohio, and as yet none of its backers has mustered the courage to attempt a rebuttal.

"Woody, who has many friends in Denver as a result of his former association with Frontier Airlines, is recognized as one of the country's most knowledgeable executives. His criticism of the SST apparently was quietly applauded by several members of the Congress, who requested copies of his speech. There were, however, no protests from those ramrodding the government-financed project. The silence seems strange since it appeared the SST ranked behind only the flag and motherhood when announced by the administration."

In his speech, Woody said that the SST has far more political than practical value and that it was unlikely to solve any problems in mass transportation.

"The airline industry and aviation-related government agencies have failed to focus sufficient attention on air and ground traffic congestion because we have been too preoccupied by speed in the wrong place."

Woody suggests that, instead of concentrating attention and dollars on the SST, the industry should built jets that take off vertically and land the same way from downtown parks on building rooftops, and that it is in this way the airlines can beat the growing airport ground-traffic congestion.

The problem of increasing ground congestion can be pointed up by a debacle that occurred at Los Angeles International Airport during a long holiday weekend not so long ago. Most flights to everywhere were booked to near capacity, yet departed with light loads. The fuming passengers who "no-showed" inched the last two miles to the airport because of a monumental traffic jam. When they did reach the airport complex, they could find no place to park their cars.

Understandably, the manufacturers are more concerned,

however, with the development and sales of new aircraft. Boeing and Douglas are building them bigger, and Lockheed, if the LST is included, is building them bigger and faster.

Another commercial air transport that Lockheed is building is known officially as the L-1011 and nicknamed by some Lockheed employees as the "Euphoria." Douglas is preparing a new aircraft known as the DC-10. Both are known to the public as "airbusses" despite the protest of the manufacturers. Boeing has its 747. It is these types of aircraft that pose a dilemma to National Airlines as well as to other carriers.

For more than a decade, the airframe manufacturers have been manufacturing subsonic jets, and the improvements have been comparatively minor. Twin-engine and tri-engine models have been introduced and then "stretched" to carry more bodies. The market for airliners is limited, and some time ago the manufacturers apparently realized that the market for jet airliners would be saturated long before an SST forced a new re-equipment program upon the airlines.

"The airframe manufacturers are copying Detroit," says Dudley Swim. "They are trying to force a re-equipment cycle by creating a style-conscious air traveler."

Woody concurs. "When the DC-3 came into being in the mid-thirties it cost about eighty-five thousand dollars and carried about twenty-one persons with reasonable utilization. It generated about nine million seat-miles a year. With the introduction of each additional model, the airlines bought more seats, more speed, better economics, and greater efficiency.

"The DC-8 'stretchout' will produce as many seat-miles in a year as fifty DC-3s, about 450 million. One airplane, costing roughly about $8½ million, cost about the same as one hundred DC-3s. But the DC-3 produced a seat-mile for approximately four cents, and a DC-8 stretchout produces a seat-mile for about a cent and a half. So we haven't become more efficient as individuals. We have purchased, through expenditures of capital funds, more efficiency.

"Now the Boeing 747," Woody continues, "will not produce

a seat-mile for much more than 5% less, yet we are talking about an airplane that will carry 385 passengers and costs $20 million. Now, let's go one step further and look at the proposed airbusses. They won't produce a seat-mile as cheap as a DC-8 stretchout.

"From the point of view of capital, we are beginning to retrogress, and our costs are going to increase. Where are we going to turn to purchase this additional efficiency?

"The supersonic jet is not going to have this efficiency for at least twenty years. When the first supersonic comes out, seat-mile costs are going to be higher than either on the airbus, the 747, or even the DC-8 stretchout.

"For the past thirty-five years, we have purchased efficiency in the airline industry. Now that we are in the subsonic age, there is no more efficiency to be purchased."

Dudley Swim expresses his views this way: "The stretched DC-8 is probably the cheapest air vehicle on the market today. There is one thing that concerns me. The aircraft manufacturers are great people and they do a great job of research, but I suspect they are deliberately starting to do what the automotive industry did long ago . . . to create obsolescence. . . . When the two-aisle plane is placed in service, is it going to make the single-aisle plane obsolete from a fashion point of view? This is what concerns me."

This attitude concerning the airbus apparently was the unanimous opinion of all of National's management. However, in an interview with Herb Shannon, aviation editor for the Long Beach *Press Telegram,* Maytag made one qualification. "If the public demands the airbus," he told Shannon, "we may be forced to join the crowd because of competitive reasons."

A short time after this, carriers competitive with National announced orders for the airbus. Evaluation teams for National began to study proposals from the two manufacturers, Douglas with its DC-10 and Lockheed with its L-1011.

Not long ago, the writer was returning to Los Angeles from

Miami on a National Airlines DC-8 powered by Pratt & Whitney engines. Seated in front of him were a young couple who appeared to be recently married.

"This is a very comfortable airplane, darling," the girl said. "What kind is it?"

The husband looked beyond her out the window. "It's a Pratt & Whitney, dear," he replied.

On another occasion, the writer was on a flight to San Francisco on a Boeing 727 listening to a seat companion explaining to a friend why he would never ride on a Boeing 727.

Most of the air-traveling public cannot tell the difference between one type of jet equipment and another. They embark and debark at most major terminals through jetways that accord them no opportunity to study the exterior of the aircraft. The interiors of all jets are so similar as to be indistinguishable to all but the most experienced airline traveler, except that some may appear longer than the others. There is a noticeable difference in the interiors of both the Boeing 747 and the airbusses. Instead of sitting six abreast, they will sit eight abreast. Instead of one aisle, there will be two, until some operator discovers that he can squeeze in ten abreast by reconfiguring the interior to one aisle.

When the subsonic jets made their debut, travelers would wait for hours, sometimes days, for the opportunity to fly in them. The airbus and the 747, however, fly at about the same speed as the first 707 or DC-8, and it is questionable whether the air traveler is going to demand a trip in an airbus in preference to more frequent scheduling by existing subsonic aircraft. There is a feeling among some airline executives that the regular, or more sophisticated, travelers may well prefer the smaller, subsonic jet, if for no other reason than that baggage handling and check-in procedures move quicker with one hundred fifty persons than they will with four hundred.

National, as well as the other trunk carriers, could not afford to proceed on this assumption, because it could well lose its percentage of the competitive market. It first ordered two of the behemoth Boeing 747s with delivery of the first scheduled in the fall of 1970, then indicated to the manufacturers that it was interested in one of the three-engined airbusses.

The competition between Lockheed and Douglas was fierce. "I awoke early one morning in Aberdeen, Washington, where I was vacationing," Woody reported, "and I found a Lockheed salesman under my bed."

There is little difference between the Lockheed and the Douglas version. The only noticeable item is that the L-1011 has an S-duct on the center engine, and the DC-10 has a straight duct with the tail mounted on top of it. They cruise at about the same rate of speed with about the same range. They have approximately the same operating cost and carry the same number of passengers.

National never officially announced why it chose the DC-10 over the Lockheed L-1011, but it can be presumed that it was primarily a matter of price. The carrier was in a situation where it could haggle, and as with automobiles, there really is no fixed price on a new airplane. The decision originally was scheduled to be made by the board of directors at a meeting in Seattle early in September of 1969. It was postponed at the last minute. An alert analyst had discovered some hidden costs that raised the price of the DC-10 about $27 million above the L-1011.

The haggling continued for another couple of weeks, in which the carrier wiped out the $27-million difference, and then National announced the purchase of nine DC-10s, with options for eight more, for about $280 million. The DC-8s presently in the fleet will be phased out, according to present plans, and probably traded in on the DC-10s. Purchase of thirteen additional DC-10s also is expected in the future.

In view of Maytag's Miami speech, however, it is unlikely that there would be any reluctance to buy Lockheed's LST if the manufacturer decides to continue with development of such an aircraft.

CHAPTER FIFTEEN

A few years ago Maytag was being interviewed in Houston, Texas, in connection with the airline's application to provide service between New Orleans and Seattle and various intermediate points. The general-assignment reporter was intelligent, but he had the attitude of many in the general public on airline operations.

"You say there is an exceptionally good growth potential on traffic between Houston and the Northwest," the reporter said. "If this is the case, why doesn't National just go ahead and fly it without government subsidy?"

"It's not quite that simple," Maytag replied patiently. "In the first place, with one exception (Northeast), there is no domestic trunk carrier within the United States that is operating under government subsidy. In the second place, there are certain ceremonial procedures that must be observed before the Civil Aeronautics Board will certify any carrier on a new route."

These ritualistic procedures that are followed by the airlines today prior to the granting of a new route are as unintelligible to most persons, both in and out of the airline industry, as are the intricate steps of a Watusi war dance.

A good example is the "route investigation," alluded to above. In 1961 National sought permission from the Civil Aeronautics Board to provide service from Houston to Seattle with stops at certain intermediate cities. A few years later, the CAB officially opened an "investigation" of the case, which was labeled the Pacific Northwest-Southwest Route Investigation and which was expanded to include terminal points at New Orleans and Seattle. The title has always remained somewhat of a mystery, since in no sweep of the imagination could New Orleans be considered to be in the Southwest. A large number of newspapers covering the case consistently assumed that "Southwest" was a typographical error and corrected it to "Southeast."

With the announcement that the case had been opened, most of the major airlines immediately applied for permission to provide service along the proposed routes. Ross Newman, a Civil Aeronautics Board examiner, was appointed to conduct the subsequent investigation. (An examiner holds a quasi-judicial position in the CAB hierarchy.)

Then the ritualistic ceremonies began. The airlines sent public-affairs men, civic-affairs men, and public-relations men scurrying from one urban area to another, trying to gather civic support and public recognition for the airlines with which they were identified. Each urban area, as does each airline, submits briefs and exhibits to the examiner stating the community's position and preference in the proposed new service. It is no longer considered good form for an urban area to mention a carrier by name as the preferred airline in the briefs filed with the examiner. The airlines prefer that the preference be shown in a more oblique manner. For example, if the city of Portland, Oregon, indicated in its brief that it was interested in the "beyond capabilities" to Miami, Florida, then it would be indicating a preference for National.

After several months of these preliminary steps in the dance, all the "interested parties" in the investigation have filed their briefs and exhibits with the examiner, with appropriate copies to each other. The next step in the ritual is the public hearing, and this is a lawyer's delight.

It is presided over by the examiner, and usually all the interested parties have counsel present to represent their interests. This mass of legal talent, usually of division strength, sits at microphone-studded tables below the examiner's podium. Behind the tables, usually in rows of folding chairs, sit the public-affairs men, the civic-affairs men, and the public-relations men, along with several high-ranking officers of the airline, often including presidents, because it is considered important that they be present to indicate to the examiner that they really are interested in the outcome of the case.

It is this part of the ritual that takes on mystic overtones. No one hears the evidence that has been presented in the briefs and exhibits that are in possession of counsel. After some bland words of welcome by various local politicians, possibly a transportation secretary of a local chamber of commerce may take the stand for cross-examination.

A lawyer is recognized by the examiner. "In your exhibit DE dash 493, subparagraph B, you say you are interested in beyond capabilities to Atlanta. Now, this does not mean that you are not equally interested in beyond capabilities to Miami, does it?"

The transportation secretary ruffles a mass of papers, then looks up. "Oh, no," he replies.

Another attorney stands. "But you definitely are interested in beyond capability to Atlanta."

"Oh, yes."

Both lawyers sit down triumphantly.

And so it continues for days, and the mass of legal minutiae accumulates. At the conclusion of the hearing, oral argument is presented in Washington and eventually the examiner retires to sift through the volumes of exhibits, evidence, and transcripts. Many months later, the examiner makes his recommendation for the carriers he believes most qualified for the route extensions according to the legal evidence collected.

The examiner's recommendations are submitted to the Civil Aeronautics Board, which sometimes follows his recommendations and just as often does not. An example of this can be cited in the Pacific Northwest-Southwest Route

Investigation. The recommendations by Newman gave the largest share of the new routes to Western Airlines. When the route awards were made some months later, Western was completely ignored, and Eastern, Continental, and Braniff were pushed from southern-midwest points into Portland and Seattle.

In the case of an international route, still another step is involved: the granting of a route certificate must be approved by the President, so, after the examiner's recommendation, there are two political hurdles that are based upon quasi-judicial procedures. An example of what can happen here can be pointed up in the results of the Trans-Pacific Route case, which was announced in two segments, late in 1968 and early in 1969. After many, many months of hearings, which ranged from Honolulu to Washington, the examiner announced his recommendations. The principal beneficiary under the recommendations was Eastern Airlines, which was extended into the South Pacific, New Zealand, and Australia.

Yet, after the recommendations went through the White House, Eastern was completely shut out, and the choice award went to Continental, whose president, Robert Six, is identified by the Los Angeles *Times* as a close friend of former President Johnson. Also receiving presidential favor was Braniff, which also enjoyed close ties to the White House.

John Cross is a Washington attorney, a member of National Airlines' board of directors, and he has been representing National in matters before the Civil Aeronautics Board since the CAB was founded, in 1938. The first case to be heard before the Board was National's petition to close the gap in its route structure between Daytona Beach and Jacksonville, Florida. John Cross was one of the attorneys representing National, and there are few who can meet his qualifications as an expert on the CAB.

"There certainly have been some politics in the award of airline routes," Cross says. "But I feel that over all there has been much less politics than the public in general really believes. These route hearings have been the basis of all companies which are existing today. Those which were able to survive financially and to acquire profitable routes, continued. The others became merged into some other airline."

The same situation exists today as did in 1938, when the airlines banded together and petitioned the federal government for federal regulation. This in itself was a political act, as were the subsidies that were paid to the carriers for more than a decade after the birth of the Civil Aeronautics Board.

Because of the subsidies, the ultimate decision after a series of route hearings had much less impact upon a carrier than it does today. If a carrier applied for a route and lost it, there was, nevertheless, still enough subsidy to keep it alive. Today, there is no subsidy for the trunks, and this, in effect, gives the CAB life-or-death control over every trunk carrier in the nation, a situation the airlines clearly did not anticipate when they conceived the idea of the CAB. The infant CAB has grown in size and become the master. If the CAB so desired, it could deny any carrier expansion and then so overload its existing routes with competition that the carrier would have no alternative but merger.

National never has been a politically oriented carrier. Baker was too abrasive to be a politician. On one occasion he publicly denounced the entire Congress of the United States as a "den of thieves." On another occasion, it is reported, he was asked to "get the hell" out of the office of Senator Smathers of Florida. On the two occasions on which he was drawn into the political arena, he came out a loser—once in the strike by the Air Line Pilots Association and the other time on the Channel 10 television imbroglio. Maytag is too candid and frank to be a man of political bent.

At a press conference, this time in Dallas, Maytag was once asked what he thought of National's chances of being certified a route in the Pacific Northwest-Southwest case.

"As a conservative Republican, I would say they are not very good," he replied. John Morris, his vice president, winced visibly.

John Cross, however, may be right in his assertion that politics plays a lesser role than the public generally believes in the granting of airline routes. National certainly never has won a route through political influence, although it lost two through its political involvement in the Channel 10 case—Chicago–Miami and St. Louis–Miami.

Baker was an admirer of the late Franklin Roosevelt, and the first route was awarded during the first Roosevelt administration, but he won it on a low bid for an airmail contract between St. Petersburg and Daytona Beach. He bid low on an airmail contract for the second route (between Jacksonville and New Orleans), as he did also when National was extended south into Miami. The connecting of the two routes, by the CAB decision to authorize National to fly between Daytona Beach and Jacksonville, was justified by the logical premise that federal subsidy would decrease if National were allowed to operate as one instead of as two separate airlines.

At the outbreak of World War II, National and the Air Transport Command contracted for National to fly an allcargo operation over its own system between Miami and New Orleans and on to Houston, Texas. It cannot be denied, however, that Washington influence was used to extend National from Miami into Key West, but the influence came from an unexpected quarter.

National had applied before the outbreak of the war to serve this resort key, but had not pursued the application aggressively because of the capital expenditures that would be required to build an airport.

Shortly after Pearl Harbor, however, the commanding officer of the U. S. Naval Base at Key West called National and asked if the carrier would provide service. He talked to Dave Amos and was told that National did have an application before the CAB for a certificate to serve Key West, but no action had been taken on it.

"His name was Reagan," Amos recalls. "He asked me who he should call, and I gave him a name. The very next day we had an order from Washington to start service into Key West. On the day after this, I was sent to Key West to look over the situation. It was an eight-hour trip by bus, over the roughest, narrowest, bumpiest road you ever saw."

Amos met with Reagan at five in the morning, was referred to a subordinate, and then inspected the salt flat with a blimp hangar that was to be the location of the Key West airport.

"By seven in the morning, we had surveyed the area and ascertained what was needed in the way of runways and buildings. I have never seen so many people work so fast in all my life. Within an hour, the place was swarming like an anthill. Before it was dark, the buildings were up and the runways completed. We started service the following day."

It is somewhat ironic that the only route segment on the National system on which pressure was applied to obtain the certificate is the segment that National has been trying unsuccessfully for years to discard. In 1954, the Monroe County Commission decided to impose a head tax of fifty cents on every passenger flying in and out of Key West, in order to improve its airport, which the Navy had built so hurriedly. Nothing offends an airline any quicker than the threat of a head tax, and Baker was no exception. He immediately cut National's schedule to Key West from four flights to one flight a day and received CAB permission for the airline to make flag stops at a wartime military field in Marathon, a growing competitive resort area on Key Vaca, about forty miles northeast of Key West. The head tax was revoked a short time later.

Today, National, whose smallest plane is a Boeing 727 jet, has tried to get permission from the CAB to turn over the Miami–Key West route to a smaller carrier, such as Southern Airways, who can provide a greater frequency of schedules between the two cities. The political pressure, however, has worked in reverse. The proposal has not been approved by the CAB.

National made the transition from a regional carrier to a major trunk carrier in 1944, when it was granted a certificate by the CAB that extended its routes from Jacksonville into New York, which at the same time gave it the New York–Miami run.

On several occasions Baker remarked that there were two incidents that made National a large carrier. "One was when I got into New York, and the other was when I got into Lehman Brothers."

There is one story in circulation that Baker was aided in the New York extension through the intervention of a Florida senator to whom Baker had lent an airplane and crew for several months during the senator's campaign for re-election. The story has received wide circulation, but it is unlikely, as the transportation would have had to occur during the war years, when air transportation was controlled by the priority system, and to take a plane out of schedule certainly would have aroused the curiosity of the military, which had lent him two of its own aircraft. Nevertheless, some old-time employees of the airline swear it is true. Others are equally vehement in their denials.

"Anyone who knew Ted, knew this wasn't true," a former National executive says. "He wouldn't have taken a plane out of service for God, although he might give him a free ride if he had an empty seat. Ted wanted those planes in the air, flying for money, all the time. He used to get mad whenever he found a plane with a cool engine."

Another story in circulation is that Baker was prompted to apply for the route by C. R. Smith of American Airlines, who, if the route award went to Baker, would then absorb National. This tale also can be discounted, as the Civil Aeronautics Board had conducted hearings on proposed additional East Coast service prior to World War II. If American had been interested at that time in a New York–Miami route, it certainly would have been an applicant in the case, but it was not. When war was declared, this case was pigeonholed.

The third story, and the most probable, is that Baker got his idea to try for New York in the same manner in which his extension into Key West was accomplished. The most powerful political force in the nation during World War II was the military. Nothing could be denied that would help the war effort, and thus, in the interests of the war effort, Baker applied for permission to extend National's routes north from Jacksonville to New York through the most restricted military areas on the East Coast. He asked for permission to serve such cities as Savannah, Charleston, Norfolk, and Wilmington. These key military areas had no direct air link with the military bases in Florida, nor with the nation's capital, nor with Philadelphia, nor with New York. Apparently the Pentagon agreed, because the route Baker asked for was awarded to National in the late summer of 1944.

"We couldn't fly it the way it was awarded," the ubiquitous Amos recalls. "So I had to go along and get permission to land at the military bases, which I got."

The real objective, however, was the New York–Miami run. Baker immediately started advertising his non-stop run between the two cities. He did not have a plane in his fleet with sufficient range to make the run non-stop, so passengers who flew National between the two cities always were faced with adverse weather conditions that demanded an unscheduled stop for refueling.

Some sixteen months later, the weather conditions improved, when Baker received his DC-4s. He immediately started non-stop service between the two cities, deeply cutting into the revenues of what had been Rickenbacker's most lucrative monopoly route. Later, in 1946, as related earlier, National was certified to fly into Havana from New York, Tampa, Miami, and Key West.

Thus, in less than a dozen years, National grew from a

nearly defunct air taxi service into a medium-sized trunk-line carrier, and this was its plateau for almost a decade and a half. It did enter into interchange agreements with Capitol, Panagra, Delta, and American, but these could not be considered as any part of a growth factor for the airline.

The interchange was the outgrowth of an idea, borrowed from the railroads, under which one plane could travel over the routes of other carriers. For example, a person going from Miami to Los Angeles could make the entire flight on one airplane. The airlines would take turns on furnishing the equipment. A National crew would fly it from Miami to New Orleans, a Delta crew on to Dallas, where an American Airlines crew would drive it the remainder of the way to Los Angeles. A similar interchange with Capitol operated between Miami, Cleveland, Buffalo, and Detroit.

There can be no question that a considerable part of the hiatus in route expansion was brought on by the CAB dismemberment proceedings against National as an outgrowth of the Air Line Pilots strike of 1948. The Board could not award route extensions to a carrier it was planning to liquidate. When this problem was eventually overcome, Baker attempted to expand National by acquisition. He was thwarted in his attempt to buy Northeast and beaten by Rickenbacker in the attempt to merge with Colonial. An earlier attempt to purchase Caribair was blocked by the CAB.

He applied for, and won, the examiner's recommendation to provide service between Chicago and Miami and between St. Louis and Miami, but this time he was blocked by the Channel 10 debacle.

To Northwest Orient went Chicago–Miami and to TWA went St. Louis–Miami. Then, early in 1961, because of the Cuban disintegration, National was forced to "temporarily suspend" service to Havana.

In fifteen years, National had not been granted any material route extension. It had been given additional competition on the New York–Miami route when the CAB put the airline Northeast into the market, and now it had lost its profitable runs to Havana.

The Northeast story is somewhat puzzling. In 1956, Northeast was given a temporary five-year certificate to fly from New York to Florida. One of the old regional carriers, Northeast had been struggling to survive even with its heavily subsidized routes in New England.

The Board, in an admitted experiment, gave Northeast the right to fly from New York to Florida on the theory that traffic on the route would increase at the same percentage rate as in the past and that by giving Northeast this extension it would eventually eliminate the carrier's $1½-million annual subsidy. The projected rate of traffic did not materialize, however, and with the advent of the jets, capacity was boosted sharply. All three airlines lost money on the route, but the greatest loser was Northeast. Its losses ran into millions. Manufacturers repossessed most of the Northeast fleet, and the airline would have collapsed had not Howard Hughes, for reasons known only to himself, dumped huge sums of money into the treasury of the sick airline.

As the expiration date of the temporary certificate drew close, the Civil Aeronautics Board decided that its experiment had not been a successful one, and it voted not to renew the Northeast certificate. In July of 1963, the CAB announced it would pay Northeast a subsidy for its regional New England operations as soon as the airline stopped operations south of New York City.

This raised a great furor around Boston, and the Justice Department, which was then headed by the late Bobby Kennedy, peculiarly intervened in behalf of Northeast. The CAB resisted the political pressure and stuck to its original decision in the Northeast case.

The next step in the affair came from the U. S. District Court in Massachusetts, when it issued an order permitting the carrier to continue its service to Florida until it could review the CAB ruling. Northeast, however, had become so destitute it couldn't continue the service. It was at this point that the CAB came up with a peculiar answer to the riddle of Northeast. It decided to subsidize the line's regional operations and suspend service on all but the most lucrative long-haul flights out of the North into Florida.

Thus, with planes furnished by Howard Hughes and operating capital by the U. S. Government, Northeast continued to remain alive. At one point, National and Eastern got together and offered to buy Northeast, with the understanding that they could shuck off the regional service to another regional carrier. The proposal was rejected by Northeast management, who later did accept an offer from Storer Broadcasting, who originally had planned to make an offer to Ted Baker for control of National.

There is a saying in the airline industry that every carrier eventually gets its "piece of pie in the sky." There is another common belief that the Civil Aeronautics Board will never let it appear that it has made a mistake. Also, if a carrier fails financially, it will reflect adversely upon the CAB itself. Whether these two theories are true is open to conjecture, but it is true that in March of 1961 National received a whopping big piece of pie when it was awarded a slice of the Southern Transcontinental Route. The route award extended National from Houston to Las Vegas and San Francisco, and to Los Angeles and San Diego.

The Southern Transcontinental Route case was a route award that had dragged on for years. It started in 1946 and became one case built on top of another, and during the entire period until it finally was settled in 1961 there was some phase of the case in process during the whole time. On the first go-around, the CAB decided that service could best be provided by an interchange agreement among Eastern, Braniff, and TWA. Under the proposal, TWA flew the segment from Los Angeles to Amarillo, Texas; Braniff, on to Houston; and Eastern, from Houston into Miami.

"We didn't like the decision," Rickenbacker says in his

memoirs, "but we went ahead and tried to make it work. An arrangement was made between TWA and Eastern to alternate with each other's planes from California to Florida. We rented Braniff's trackage from Amarillo to Houston."

In the days prior to the inauguration of this service, full-page ads appeared in all the daily newspapers between the two points. Two days before the service was scheduled to start, Eastern launched a pre-inaugural flight from Miami to Los Angeles. Newsmen and VIPs were taken on board at Miami, New Orleans, Houston, Amarillo, and other communities, flown to the Southern California city, and taken to the huge Biltmore Hotel for a banquet that was to climax the celebration over the pending service.

Baker disliked the whole idea even more than his rival Rickenbacker. As soon as the newspaper ads appeared, Baker met with John Cross, and Cross found a great, big flaw in the Board's decision to set up the interchange.

The ballroom at the Biltmore was full of dignitaries from California to Florida. The dessert was on the table, and Rickenbacker was getting ready to speak when an aide approached him on the dais and handed him a telegram. Baker had been granted an injunction by the federal court prohibiting the inauguration of the interchange. A stunned Rickenbacker read the telegram to his assembled guests and on the following day flew back to Miami, dropping off his VIPs on the way.

"In this first Southern Transcontinental Route case, the interchange routing had never been an issue," Cross says. "I had never heard of it until after the Board had awarded it, so we had no chance to oppose it. After the court granted the injunction, the matter was sent back to the Board for reconsideration."

Rickenbacker says that Baker "was prompted by American," but American Airlines had nothing to do with it. One Los Angeles paper headlined the incident, "RICK SHOT OUT OF THE AIR."

On its second consideration, the CAB again came up with

the interchange idea for service along the Southern Transcontinental Route, but this time three different carriers were named. National was to fly the Miami–New Orleans segment; Delta, on to Dallas; and American Airlines, on through Phoenix to Los Angeles. The airlines worked out their own agreements on the equipment, but it was always single-plane service. This service remained in effect until the case was finally resolved in 1961. If National had not been given a portion of the award, it is quite probable that the airline would have been swallowed by some other carrier in the early sixties.

There is an attitude prevalent among many airline executives that the CAB is inclined to reward an inefficiently run carrier by granting it route extensions. Neither Bud Maytag, Ray Woody, nor John Cross accepts this theory.

"We have argued," Cross says, "that the reward for efficiency is competition. After a carrier has developed a route to the point where it is strong, the CAB takes a look at it and says, 'This is a very profitable route and it will support two carriers.' Therefore the reward for developing traffic and increasing service is to get competition.

"A good example of this is the New York–Florida route," Cross continues. "For several years, National and Eastern developed this route, and I honestly believe National made the greatest contribution. National organized the hotels to give reduced rates during the summer, and it reduced fares in order that people would vacation there during the summer as well as the winter. After National and Eastern developed the traffic into a year-round flow, the Board decided it was time for a third carrier and put in Northeast."

In 1961, National showed a loss of $7¼ million despite six months of operation on the Southern Transcontinental Route, and even the affluent Eastern became so poor it tried desperately to merge with American.

National, ever since 1961, has operated in the black, and there is no doubt that this is because of the Southern Transcontinental Route. The route was a monopoly on a few segments only: California–Florida, Las Vegas–Houston, and San Francisco–Houston, and the average load factor on the entire route was 50%.

Despite this low load factor, however, the CAB, in mid-1969, placed several other carriers into the market, thus shoring up the theory that the reward for efficiency is increased competition. Northeast was extended from Miami to Los Angeles. American was placed in the Houston–San Francisco market, and Delta was granted Miami–San Francisco authority. In the same decision, National was placed in competition with Delta on a non-stop Atlanta–San Francisco run, a route that Delta had been serving as a monopoly since 1961.

Although this saturation of the Southern Transcontinental Route will result in financial loss to National, the losses will be offset considerably by another award made by the CAB in 1969, when it gave to National the long-coveted non-stop route between Miami, Florida, and London, England, in competition with BOAC.

Although National is not a politically oriented carrier, as stated earlier, it is interesting to trace the parallel between National's route expansion and the Republican and Democratic administrations. The present unabashed and candid management team of National assumed control four months after the late President Kennedy came into power. Since that time and continuing through the administration of President Johnson, National was the only trunk carrier in the nation that was not awarded some route expansion. It was recommended by an examiner for a route to Nassau, Bahamas, from the West Coast of the United States, but this was denied. It lost its lucrative interchange between New York and Miami, after Braniff bought Panagra and was allowed to extend its routes up the East Coast. This cost National an estimated $2 million annually in operating revenues.

In the muddled Trans-Pacific case, the two Democratic-oriented carriers, Continental and Braniff, fared well under the Johnson recommendations, but the timing was somewhat off. In a case involving international routes, the final decision is made by the President. The CAB examiner has recommended that Eastern be given most of the Pacific as far as Australia, and Hawaii from most of the urban areas in the South. Johnson overruled the CAB and gave Australia to Continental, and Hawaii from the southern cities and Mexico to Braniff.

The Johnson decision was announced December 19, thirty-two days before he was scheduled to leave the White House. The carriers that received no awards had, by law, twenty days to petition for a reconsideration of the case and an additional ten days for filing answers. The actual thirty-day period expired on a Saturday, but precedent and rules of practice state that when Saturday is the end of a period, the allowable time is extended until the following Monday. Monday was the day of inauguration of the incoming President and thus was a legal holiday in the District of Columbia. The CAB could not meet on a legal holiday, apparently. Here, again, precedent and the rules of practice put off the deadline for an additional day. But by this time Richard Nixon was President and it was up to him, not Johnson, to determine the route awards in an international case. The CAB apparently realized that Johnson had miscalculated, and it then extended the filing deadline for an additional two days. Within these two days, Nixon recalled the entire case for further study.

That he was justified in so doing is evidenced by the criticism from the nation's aviation press of the original Johnson decision. The charges ranged from "cronyism" to "politics-ridden and sloppy." *Aviation Daily* explained the Johnson boner. "Confusion has reigned supreme in the Pacific considerations of CAB for twenty years. The present jumbo case is no exception. This time the pressures were enormous and instead of one man in the White House assigned to handle the case for the President there were too many by far. . . . The transpacific case probably will be around for some time yet."

The Civil Aeronautics Board consists of five persons, and by law it must have two members of each political party. When Nixon was inaugurated, the CAB was made up of three Democrats and two Republicans. One of the Democrats was the CAB chairman, John J. Crooker, a Johnson appointee and member of a Houston law firm that handled some of Johnson's interests.

Nixon sent the case back to the CAB, recommending, in essence, that the CAB consider a carrier that could provide service to the South Pacific from the eastern seaboard. The recommendation generally was interpreted as favoring Eastern, the carrier that originally had been recommended for the route.

The Democratic-oriented CAB came back with Continental again, however, this time granting the carrier the rights to serve Australia from Washington, D.C. It was a peculiar proposal, as Continental did not serve any city east of Chicago or New Orleans. In order to service this route, Continental would have to be granted a domestic extension on which no hearings had been held and which certainly would have been challenged by other carriers on the same grounds as Baker had challenged the Eastern interchange award several years earlier.

A couple of weeks after this recommendation was made, Continental applied for permission to fly between Chicago and Washington, but the gesture was futile because Nixon once again rejected the CAB recommendations, pointing out that New York also was located on the eastern seaboard.

The press generally interpreted this once again as Nixon support for Eastern. The CAB sent back its next recommendation—for American Airlines to serve the South Pacific—and this was signed by the President. Expanded authority across the Pacific also was given to Northwest, Pan American, and TWA. Flying Tiger was granted an all-cargo route.

A short time later, the CAB announced its awards in the domestic portion of the Trans-Pacific case—service between the mainland and Hawaii. Eight airlines were authorized to serve the resort islands from almost every metropolitan area in the United States. The carriers are Western, United, TWA, Pan American, Northwest, Continental, Braniff, and American. With such heavy competition, it will be a long time before any carrier finds the route very profitable.

National did not pursue any international routes in the Trans-Pacific case. It did seek authority to serve Hilo and Honolulu from the California gateways and cities along its Southern Transcontinental Route.

The carrier still is seeking additional domestic authority. Among the routes sought are service between the Pacific Northwest and California, and non-stop service between Salt Lake City and San Francisco to the west and Chicago, Washington, and New York to the east.

The airline has a professional optimist named Milt Heilbrun as station manager in Los Angeles. Heilbrun has been employed by National for many years. "When we lost Chicago and St. Louis, I felt bad," he says. "When we lost Havana I got sick. But if we hadn't lost Chicago, St. Louis, and Havana, we would never have got Los Angeles, so it always comes out better."

"What about these new carriers the CAB has put on the Southern Transcontinental Route?"

"That's bad," Heilbrun says. "But then we got London. That's how the system works."

Maytag believes that one of the problems that faces any corporation under rigid control of a federal regulatory agency is that current conditions simply outstrip the facts of record.

"There is no denying the fact that management, through its lawyers, is responsible for a part of the time-consuming delay in regulatory law. We play for big stakes in the federally regulated fields. Millions upon millions of dollars ride on the outcome of a proceeding. To some corporations, the grant or denial of a certificate is a matter of life and death. Who, under these circumstances, would dare leave a stone unturned, would submit a brief without covering every facet, would dare not petition for reconsideration or prosecute an appeal no matter how small his chances? Although lawyers may take the brunt of the criticism because they are so intimately involved in proceedings, it is hardly fair criticism if the delay arises as a result of a lawyer doing his best to protect the interests of his client."

Sometimes these delays have peculiar results. When John Cross secured his injunction against Rickenbacker in the first Southern Transcontinental Route case, it probably was intended as a delaying tactic to enable Baker to have another crack at the route. It is unlikely that either Baker or Cross or Rickenbacker thought that the action would really throw Eastern entirely out of the market and eventually give it to National.

There is another example. During the mid-1950s, the Civil Aeronautics Board instituted a number of large route cases that culminated in additional multicarrier competition. For the most part, its decisions were based upon the traffic-generating ability of piston-engine equipment.

Coincidentally with the decision of the case, the jet age arrived, and the airlines entered a period of recession brought on by overcapacity. The route decision was based upon outdated records and questionable forecasts.

"If time is the sole standard for measuring the effectiveness of the legal process," Maytag says, "then regulatory law and lawyers have not and cannot keep pace with those they seek to serve and protect."

Maytag adds, however, that time and expediency cannot be the sole criteria for determining the need for change in the system.

But this is how the system works.

CHAPTER SIXTEEN

One of the legacies that Baker left was the reputation that National was plagued by labor problems. It was a reputation that was undeserved and undoubtedly stemmed from the highly publicized pilots' strike of 1948, which almost put the airline out of business. Actually, National has had fewer strikes than most carriers, and its contracts with the several unions represented on the payroll pay nearly the highest, if not the highest, in the industry.

In the beginning, there were no unions, which was indeed fortunate for Baker, as he had no money with which to pay his workers. Kershaw's starting salary was approximately one hundred dollars a month. Dave Amos remembers that when he finally did go on a payroll, he would run like hell to get his check cashed while there still was some money in the bank. "If you made it," he recalls, "the chances were pretty good that Baker would immediately borrow it back from you."

All of the carriers in the United States are now heavily unionized, with the exception of Pacific Southwest Airlines and Delta. The latter carrier has union pilots, but the rest of its personnel belong to no union. It keeps the union out by paying a higher salary. This gets into the endless discussion as to whether workers prefer higher salaries over job security provided by unions and whether companies prefer unions, with the resulting millions of dollars saved in payroll costs but with the recurring threat of strikes. These relationships exist in most industries.

A unique problem with the airline, and all airlines, is in the relationship between management and the all-powerful Air Line Pilots Association. The pilots like to think of ALPA as an organization somewhat similar to the American Bar Association or the American Medical Association. Their income exceeds that of many doctors and lawyers.

Trans World Airlines, for example, has already reached an agreement with its pilots on the salary to be paid to a captain of a Boeing 747, which will be flying shortly and carrying close to five hundred passengers. The basic salary that TWA will pay a captain is $55,000 a year. In addition to this, TWA will contribute about 25% of a captain's annual salary into his pension fund, which will give him an annual income of approximately $67,500. For this, he will work only 85 hours a month.

A pilot now earns about $37,500 annually, counting the pension contributions, which approximates the annual salary of a number of the airlines' vice presidents.

The incongruity of the situation is that a professional man deals on a person-to-person basis and establishes rates of pay that are commensurate with the particular job he does at his particular abilities. In the airline industry, the poor pilot is paid as much as the good pilot, and sometimes, depending upon seniority, a poor pilot is paid more than a good pilot.

A few months after Maytag took over National, the Air Line Employees Association struck the carrier. Woody does not know whether the union was testing the new management or whether the strike was the result of a hard approach by the ALEA executives because of a threatened raid by the Teamsters.

"Their union was not too large and it had been raided successfully before," he says.

It is a situation that is not peculiar to the airline. The executives of a union must keep promising in order to maintain the support of the membership. National was caught in this bind, but the strike lasted less than 24 hours and the new contract provided sufficient benefits to prevent the ALEA membership from turning to the Teamsters.

During the summer of 1967, National was one of six of the nation's trunk carriers that were shut down because of a summer-long strike by the International Association of Machinists. Then again, in January 1969, the IAM union members in New York, Miami, and Newark pulled a wildcat strike for which there is no logical answer.

It started on January 17 at John F. Kennedy International Airport, when three IAM members employed by National were suspended for refusing to taxi an aircraft with a two-man crew. The major carriers at New York, such as American, Braniff, Delta, Northwest, Pan American, and United, all use two-man ground crews to taxi aircraft from the gates to parking areas and hangars. National had been using three men, but many weeks earlier had discontinued this practice to conform to the industry-wide procedure of using two men.

On the day of the walkout, P. L. Siemiller, the president of the IAM, wired National, "The action on the part of your employees was not and is not approved or sanctioned by Grand Lodge, District Lodge 145, or the local lodges."

Despite this disclaimer, however, some eleven hundred union members remained off the job in the three cities. The following day, the U. S. District Court in Miami granted a preliminary injunction against the union that ordered the workers to return to their jobs and directed National to use three men to taxi aircraft until the court had made a determination of the issue. The members of the IAM who had walked off the job ignored the court order.

Two days later, the same court held another hearing and ruled that the union members had not returned to work and that the union leaders "had not taken all available steps necessary to accomplish this end." The federal judge said also, ". . . it is the order of this Court and of the defendant IAM that all men return to work by their next shift and that individuals who refuse to so report are subject to penalties which could include dismissal by National Airlines."

The IAM sent telegrams to its members telling them to go back to work or face possible dismissal, and at the same time other union members gathered in the parking lots and around the hangars threatening those members who did appear for work.

National waited an additional twenty-four hours, also sent telegrams to the striking employees asking them to return, then when they failed to return, fired all the approximately eleven hundred men participating in the wildcat strike. There was some violence in Miami. Workers who wanted to return to work reported that bricks had been thrown through the windows of their homes, or their cars had been damaged. But nowhere else in National's system did the IAM members leave their jobs. No other union respected the picket lines at either New York or Miami. National launched a massive recruitment program, and mechanics poured into Miami from San Diego, Los Angeles, Chicago, and other cities. Management personnel, up to vice presidents, worked nights cleaning the planes.

"He's a better cleaner than the professionals," one stewardess said admiringly of a vice president.

Unlike the debacle of 1948, National found that public support was behind the company, as well as its other union employees. Newspaper editorials commended the carrier for its stand.

". . . employers probably are fearful of political authorities which, like the Maryland legislature, appear to bend over backward to guard the alleged rights of unions, but sometimes seem not to think that employers and the public have any rights at all," *The Wall Street Journal* said in commending National's stand in the illegal strike.

In a West Coast city, an IAM representative was bluntly

told to leave the premises when he sought support for "our striking brothers in Miami."

By the end of February, more than 850 persons had been employed in New York and Miami. Some of them were men who had reluctantly gone out on the wildcat strike. Although less in number, the new men apparently were more efficient, because a couple of weeks later service was virtually back to normal on National's system.

There is a reason for the *esprit de corps* among most of National's employees. After the brief ALEA strike in 1962, plans were drawn up that would enable the company to compete effectively with the unions for the loyalty of its employees. A supervisory training program was inaugurated in which the union, or contract, employees were afforded a chance to move up into supervisory positions. It was discovered that the policy of delegation of authority subscribed to by Maytag and Woody was not filtering down to the lower levels of management because of the long years of conditioning under the Baker regime.

Union men who had been hard-nosed about the union were equally as hard-nosed about the company when they were promoted to foreman or supervisor. At the same time, a problem that could be solved at a ticket counter by an on-the-spot decision by a senior agent was being bucked upstairs to a station manager who in turn passed it on to the general office, a standard operating procedure under the previous management. The problem still exists, but nowhere to the extent that it had before the advent of the new management.

In labor relations, all airline managements' area of control has steadily narrowed. Airline employees consistently have enjoyed preferential treatment over other unions. They are allowed compulsory unionism, since the Railway Labor Act governs contract negotiations with the airlines as well as with the railroads.

The Act is administered by the National Mediation Board. The statute requires that every railroad, every air carrier, and their employees establish a system board to provide for a prompt and orderly settlement of disputes growing out of grievances or interpretation of contracts.

If negotiations between an airline and a union are not successful, the Mediation Board then can be asked to intervene and may proffer its services. If mediation fails, the Board tries to induce the parties to submit their controversy to arbitration. Then, if arbitration is refused by either party, usually comes the strike.

There is a final step that can be taken by government, and this is the appointment of a Presidential Emergency Board. The strength and value of an Emergency Board's recommendations are derived from the prestige of the President of the United States, but the findings are not binding on either party.

Many of the airlines are party to an agreement that, if one of the carriers is struck, competing carriers will share their increase in operating revenues with the struck carrier. At one time, National was party to this agreement, but the carrier withdrew after it underwent a brief strike and Baker thought Eastern should have paid over a lot larger amount than it did. Several months later, Eastern was struck and Baker gleefully banked the profits garnered at the expense of Rickenbacker.

When written into law, the Railway Labor Act was hailed as a model statute for preventing strikes, but it has not worked out that way. Instead, it has compressed the area in which airline management has a right to run its business. An example of this is a recent federal court ruling that employers must bargain with the unions on the question of subcontracting work presently done in the company's own shops.

"No one in airline management expects trade unions to go away," Maytag said in a speech at Los Angeles Town Hall. "All of us recognize that we have an obligation to labor, as well as to the public and to the stockholders. But we do each of these groups a disservice if we allow the airlines to stagnate as have the railroads."

There has been only one other strike against National since

Maytag came onto the scene. National was one of five carriers struck for forty-one days in 1966 by the International Association of Machinists.

It is inevitable that there will be others.

Another problem that faced Maytag was the "tin shack" facilities still in use at New York's Kennedy Airport. At first it was planned to build a new terminal adjacent to the elongated Quonset hut, but this would have been too easy.

At most airports in the United States, the carriers work together in their negotiations with airport management, but the New York Port Authority had adopted the practice of dealing with each airline separately. In this manner, the Port Authority played one carrier against the other. When the problem arose over the proposed fourth New York airport, C. R. Smith of American Airlines proposed that all the carriers serving New York band together to form a Metropolitan Airport Council. The theory behind this was that the airlines eventually would pay for the airport through leases and landing fees and other similar costs, and they therefore should work as a cohesive unit.

Ray Woody accepted the invitation to join MAC on behalf of National. Almost immediately, National's plans to build a modern terminal building became snagged by the Port Authority. It accepted the plans and then refused to either approve or reject them. The engineering staff at National drew up additional plans and specifications to modernize the "tin shack" and these plans were filed on top of the others. No action was taken.

After many months, a frustrated Ray Woody tackled the problem from a different angle. He approached some of the other carriers at the airport with the suggestion that National lease a portion of their facilities. Although the carriers approached were non-competitive, the reaction to this proposal was universally negative.

There was only one direction left in which to turn. National formally withdrew its membership from the Metropolitan Airport Council. Two days later, the Port of New York Authority approved not only the plans for the new terminal, but also those for the temporary improvements to Baker's tin shack.

A reporter called a spokesman for the New York Port Authority and bluntly asked if there was any relationship between the Port Authority's approval of the plans and National's withdrawal from MAC.

"Pure coincidence," was the reply.

The new multimillion-dollar National Terminal at Kennedy Airport opened in late 1969.

A similar facility-expansion program by the airline also was snagged in Miami some time later. Here it was the practice of the Dade County Port Authority to issue revenue bonds that would finance such expansion projects. Because they were revenue bonds, and would be paid for by National, they would cost the taxpayers nothing. Nevertheless, a local attorney filed suit to prevent the expansion program, and it was held up for several months until it was rejected by the courts.

From their formative years until the advent of the jets, the airlines of the United States were identified with personalities. These personalities usually were the presidents, and they were treated as celebrities. There are very few among the general public who can name the president of U. S. Steel or of General Motors, yet until very recently most persons were aware of the man who ran an airline. Rickenbacker meant Eastern Airlines, and Eastern Airlines meant Rickenbacker; Howard Hughes meant TWA; Juan Trippe meant Pan American, and Ted Baker meant National.

With one or two exceptions, this no longer is the case. The Hugheses, Trippes, and Rickenbackers no longer run their airlines. The presidents work on "contracts" from the carriers' boards of directors, and there is a uniform, faceless quality that conforms to standards demanded by the banks and insurance companies who control the carriers. Understandably, the management of most carriers run their airlines for the benefit of management rather than their stockholders, because the stockholdings are so widely spread that control of the carrier is not held by management.

National is one of the exceptions. The control is held by Maytag and Swim, the president and the chairman of the board, and thus, being major stockholders, they are more consistently aware of stockholder interests than their counterparts in some of the other carriers. Because of this, they are also relieved of many of the restrictive, conforming demands imposed upon their counterparts.

Thus, National still is an airline with a colorful personality, because it is run by persons who are not forced to conform to a colorless image. Maytag is the nucleus of National, as was Baker before he left. He has a reputation in the airline of forgetting nothing, and he will listen to anyone. Sometimes he will nod and explain the reasons for a situation or a problem that is brought to his attention by a ramp agent, or a stewardess, or a vice president. On other occasions he will jot the problem down in a tiny notebook he carries with him, and this means he will investigate the problem or the situation as soon as possible. Most of the employees watch Maytag carefully to see if he pulls out his notebook. It has become a symbol.

On one occasion in Los Angeles, he was leaving a DC-8 and noticed that the "V" had disappeared from the word "lavatory" on one of the forward "blue rooms." He made a notation in his notebook, and one of the station agents who had boarded the aircraft noticed it. When he returned to the operations office, he suggested to one of the maintenance men that the missing letter be restored before the plane departed on another flight.

"Where in hell am I going to get a V in Los Angeles?" the maintenance man asked.

"Maytag wrote it down."

"Okay, we'll find a V."

When someone reported the incident to Maytag later, he

laughed. "I was wondering why we were putting letters on the door that will fall off," he explained.

Unlike Baker, his antecedents are extremely well known. He is a great-grandson of a man who migrated to Iowa from the Frankfurt area of Germany and who, through the development of an extremely efficient washing machine, made his name a household word the world over. His childhood was not an exceptional one. Once, when a young boy, he rode to Chicago in an old Ford tri-motor plane. "When I got out of that," he says, "if anyone had told me that I would make a career out of aviation, I would have thought him to be out of his mind."

Both he and his family thought he had an unusual talent for music, and his very early training was with this in mind, but this bent proved to be of a temporary nature. When he was still young, he was brought to Colorado Springs by his parents, where he attended high school and started a degree course in business at Colorado College. However, he temporarily set this aside when he became eligible for the draft, in order to join the Air Force, and it was at this time that he acquired his lasting interest in aviation. It had been his intention to learn the art of flying while in the Air Force, but he was discharged from the service during the heavy demobilization of the armed forces in late 1945. He returned to college, but concurrently earned a pilot's license at a nearby flying school. He has never stopped learning. Today, he is qualified to fly every type of aircraft in National's fleet and has been checked out by Lockheed as a pilot in the supersonic Starfighter.

When Maytag learned to fly, the era of the barnstormers was long gone and every facet of aviation was becoming business-oriented. The helmets and goggles were as remote from the fixed-base operators as they were in the commercial airlines. Maytag liked to fly aerobatically, but as a sport only. Because he was both business- and aviation-oriented, it is understandable that his first company, formed when he was twenty-two years old, combined both of these interests under the name of Maytag Aircraft Corporation. The company was formed with the purpose of operating a flying school at Peterson Field in Colorado Springs.

When the Korean War broke out, however, the Air Force once again took over the operation of Peterson Field, and Maytag steered his fledgling company in a new direction by bidding successfully for an Air Force refueling contract at the airport. Within a very short time, the Maytag Aircraft Corporation had burgeoned into an international organization with Air Force refueling contracts that at one time included fifteen bases inside the United States, one in Bermuda, and three in Germany.

In 1958, about the time that Baker was first sounding out Continental on merger plans, Maytag heard that Frontier was having financial trouble, and the idea occurred to him to go into the airline business. At that time, Frontier was a much smaller regional carrier than it is today, and throughout the Rocky Mountain West, where it principally operated, it had the unenviable reputation of being known as an aerial "Toonerville Trolley." Its owners were delighted to sell out control to Maytag for eight hundred thousand dollars. At the time, Maytag was thirty-two years old.

"I didn't know anything about airlines," Maytag readily admits, "so I didn't immediately walk in there and try to run Frontier. I went in as chairman of the board and did nothing but watch it for a while."

By the end of the year, Maytag knew, ". . . it wasn't going right. Someone had to take it over and shake it up." He turned first to Robert Six, president of Continental, which, at that time, also was headquartered in Denver.

"He had an executive vice president who had just retired. The man was fairly young, and I thought he might be interested in the job. He wasn't. He said he would find someone, but he didn't."

By January of 1959, Maytag still had found no one he felt

was qualified for the presidency of Frontier, so he took over the job himself. He continued his search for expert help.

At this time, Frontier had an attorney in Washington named Harry Bowen who was handling the route work for the carrier before the Civil Aeronautics Board. During the early part of 1959, Maytag was in Bowen's office and mentioned that he needed an expert executive vice president. Bowen replied that he knew of a man who might be interested, a G. Ray Woody, who presently held a similar position with TACA, an airline serving most of the Central American nations.

Woody indeed was an expert in the airline industry.

A native of Patrick County, Virginia, Woody had first been exposed to flying when he was twelve years old, when a cousin taught him the rudimentary rules of handling an aircraft. In 1935, he enrolled in Spartan College, in Tulsa, Oklahoma, a college with a limited curriculum but one that did include courses in flying. These courses undoubtedly were included because of a very close relationship financially with the company that manufactured Spartan aircraft.

The course was brief and jobs were scarce, and after his graduation, Woody raised what funds he could for the purchase of a secondhand Spartan and set out on a barnstorming tour of the United States. He did not get very far. On one of his early flights, his engine failed on take-off and the plane was demolished in the ensuing crash, although Woody escaped with minor injuries. He then was employed by the Piper Aircraft Corporation in Lock Haven, Pennsylvania, moved on to a flying and charter service in Charleston, West Virginia, and from there as an instructor with the Twin Cities Flying Service in Cincinnati, Ohio. It was in this city, in about 1939, that he met an executive from TWA during a lunch and was offered a job, which he accepted, as a pilot for TWA.

Woody flew for TWA until the outbreak of the war, when he joined the Navy as a pilot. It was here that the chain of events began that eventually pulled Woody from a cockpit to an executive's chair, although he still is an avid acrobatic flier.

When the war ended, Woody had three alternatives: he was offered a permanent commission in the Navy, an opportunity to return to TWA, and a captain's position with Waterman Airlines, an offshoot of the Waterman Steamship Company, which was trying to obtain CAB permission to fly from the United States mainland into Puerto Rico. In order to prove their capability in an airline operation, Waterman Airlines had established an intrastate carrier in Alabama.

Woody turned down the offer of a permanent commission in the Navy and reported back to TWA. "They were having at this time some internal trouble with the pilots because of difficulties on the seniority list and it appeared that a strike might occur. I had ninety days to do almost anything before I lost my seniority, so I went down to Mobile to look into the Waterman operation."

What Woody saw at Waterman, he liked. He started out as a captain and within five months had moved up through chief pilot to vice president. Everyone at Waterman was confident that it was destined to become a major carrier and that there would be no problem with the Civil Aeronautics Board in acquiring a certificate to fly between New Orleans and San Juan. Unfortunately, everyone at Waterman was overly optimistic. The Puerto Rico route was given to Chicago & Southern, which later was absorbed by Delta, and Waterman found itself flying expensive DC-4 equipment on short intrastate hops in Alabama.

At this time, TACA was partially owned by TWA, and TACA was losing so much money that TWA wanted to get rid of its interest in it. Waterman bought out the TWA interest, abandoned its unprofitable intrastate Alabama service, and took over the operation of TACA, keeping its name. Ray Woody moved to New Orleans as executive vice president of the new operation. He took with him as his vice president of traffic and sales a young man named J. Dan Brock. In 1959, Ray Woody still was executive vice president of TACA.

"I was introduced to Bud Maytag over the telephone by Harry Bowen, and then he came down to New Orleans. He was in no fog over what he wanted to do, and I was in a dead end at TACA. We didn't negotiate very long. We had a meeting of the minds almost at once."

Early in 1959, G. Ray Woody moved to Denver to become executive vice president of Frontier Airlines. A short time later, Dan Brock moved up from TACA to Frontier to fill the position of vice president of traffic and sales. The future management team of National Airlines was beginning to meld.

Brock has spent all of his life in the airline industry. He went to work for Eastern Airlines in 1939 in Montgomery, Alabama, as a combination agent, about the same time that Baker began baiting Rickenbacker. A combination agent in 1939 was required to have a first-class radio license, refuel planes, unload and load baggage, sell tickets, and check in the passengers. Brock quite candidly admits he had little interest in aviation before he went to work for Eastern. "It was the first job I could get during the depression after I got out of school," he says.

With the advent of World War II, he enlisted in the Army Air Corps, was graduated from Officer Candidate School, and then was assigned to the Air Transport Command under C. R. Smith, on leave from American Airlines; he was assigned to stations both within the United States and in Europe. Upon his discharge, in 1945, he returned to Alabama, met Ray Woody, and joined Waterman Airlines.

Waterman Airlines was owned by the Waterman Steamship Company, and the airline was formed with the purpose of getting a route from New York to San Juan. Trial runs were made between the two cities and, coincidentally, the chief pilot on these runs was National's E. J. Kershaw, who was given a leave of absence by Baker for these trips.

Kershaw recalls Baker's comment, "If Waterman is successful, we might be able to make a deal with them some day."

Waterman was not successful. Its first bid for the route was rejected on the ground that it lacked experience as a carrier. Officials of the company combated this by starting their intra-state service in Alabama with a fleet consisting of Lockheed Lodestars, DC-3s, and two DC-4s. Such a fleet in a compara-tively small state could not hope to operate profitably, but it did build up an experience factor. When Waterman applied once again for the New York–San Juan route, it learned that the CAB disapproved of steamship companies owning airlines. As proof it cited the recent divorce of American Overseas Airlines from American Export Lines. (AOA was absorbed by Pan American.) It was then that Waterman decided to buy TWA's interest in TACA, which covered most of Central America. TWA was losing approximately $7 million annually on the operation, which was a loosely knit organization of several Central American carriers.

It was a lateral move for Brock and Woody. Woody moved in as executive vice president and Brock as vice president of traffic and sales. The two men immediately began to stream-line the organization in an attempt to put it on a profitable basis. Some of the non-productive routes were discarded, in-cluding a run across the Gulf of Mexico to Miami. Affiliated companies that were losing money were severed from the parent organization. It was not done easily.

On one occasion, Brock and Woody were in San Salvador attending a reception when a discharged sales representative appeared with a gun in his hand and announced that he was there to shoot Brock. Ray Woody intercepted the irate sales-man and deftly took the revolver away from him.

On another occasion, Brock went to the airport of a Central American country to meet a foreign dignitary, with plans to take him to dinner. The invitation was declined and Brock departed for his hotel. The next morning he learned that four would-be assassins had been arrested immediately outside the airport terminal building. Their intended victim was the same man Brock had planned to take to dinner, and had the invita-tion been accepted, National's management team would have a different vice president of sales from the one it has today, as Brock surely would have been gunned down with the VIP.

When Brock moved into the Frontier organization, he did the same thing he was to do later with National. He increased the sales staff fourfold. Frontier only had six outside salesmen for its entire system. In some cities, he discovered, one man was still operating in the same manner as Brock had when he started with Eastern in 1939.

"I found out that, where we had routes which were competitive with the trunks, it was easy to outsell them when we put a salesman in the territory. In some cities, such as Albuquerque, Tucson, and Phoenix, we found travel agents who had never had a sales representative call upon them. Promotional and excursion fares were instituted. Frontier almost at once began to show an increase in operating revenues."

The greatest increase came from travel agents. The same philosophy is applied today to National, which derives more of its total business from travel agents than any other trunk carrier. It has kept National operating in the black and it has given Brock a nickname among the salesmen throughout the system. He is known as "Calls Brock."

Brock has another function in the hierarchy than sales. This is the catchall of "traffic." In one aspect, traffic is an operational matter, but in another, it includes all persons who have a direct contact with the public, such as ticket agents, reservations departments, and in-flight services such as stewardesses and catering. Advertising programs also fall under this jurisdiction.

Two more key executives were added to the Frontier management team shortly after the arrival of Brock and Woody. These were Edward J. Dolansky, vice president of finance, who came to the carrier from the Minneapolis-Honeywell Corporation, and William A. Nelson, who financed his studies through law school by working as an airline ticket agent, and now is a vice president and general counsel for the airline.

Dolansky, soft-spoken and quiet, has been referred to on various occasions as "a financial genius" by Maytag, Swim, and Truex. When National placed its first order for the Boeing 727, a purchase of thirteen jets, a Boeing executive was congratulated for finally getting Boeing equipment into the National fleet.

"You'd better hold off on the accolades," the executive replied wryly. "By the time Ed Dolansky got through re-writing the contract, I think we lost money."

Nelson has a strong sense of humor that covers an innate shyness, and, like many corporate attorneys, he shuns publicity. "Lawyers most often get into trouble when they speak into a microphone that is attached to some form of a recording device," he once told the writer. He is, however, gregarious and disarming, and he has a phenomenal memory, which is a decided asset for any attorney.

This was the group that trained as a team for more than three years at Frontier Airlines, the group that was put together by Maytag and brought by him from Frontier to National.

Officers who had been with National and survived the transition include M. C. (Steve) Wedge, vice president of flight operations; Jerome (Jerry) Rosenthal, vice president of industrial relations; Harry Taylor, vice president of properties, and John L. Morris, who recently partially retired and was appointed a special consultant to the company. After Morris' retirement, Elmer E. Jones, Jr., a veteran of many years' service with TWA, joined the National officer ranks with the title of vice president of public affairs. All these men are experts in their fields, a fact attested to by the positions they hold.

The career of Steve Wedge for many years ran parallel to that of Ray Woody. Like Woody, Wedge was born in West Virginia and started flying as a young man. About the time Woody went to training school in Oklahoma, Wedge enrolled in a similar school in Oakland, California. When Woody joined TWA as a pilot, Wedge became a pilot for United. With the outbreak of World War II, however, Woody went into the Navy, and Wedge became a ferry pilot flying bombers to Europe and Africa under contract to Pan American. When Woody was barnstorming as an acrobatic pilot in West Virginia, Wedge was attempting to break the world's solo endurance record on "the other side of the mountains." He did not break the record, but he lost the hairs on his head.

He took off at 3:30 on an early-summer afternoon over a potato festival in southern Ohio, just across the border from West Virginia. He had enough fuel on board to fly until the next morning. The art of refueling in the air had not been well developed at this time, and the way Wedge met this problem was to come in low over a deserted field, catch a two-gallon can of fuel with a grappling hook, pull it in, then climb back to an altitude where the plane would fly by itself long enough to allow Wedge time to dump the contents of the can into the fuel tank. It took him most of the day to pick up enough fuel to enable him to fly through the following night. Shortly before dawn the next morning, an oil line in the cockpit cracked. He tried to patch it and thought he had succeeded.

The last thing he remembers about the flight is seeing the sun appear on the horizon. The airplane spiraled down and crashed in a West Virginia orchard. When it hit the first tree, the impact tore off a wing, and broke open the cabin door and the safety belt, spilling Wedge out on the ground. He was in the hospital for six weeks, and when he left, there was not a hair left on his head. He is not the least bit sensitive about it.

Not long ago, a mechanic in Los Angeles commented that Wedge's head was as "smooth as my girl's fanny."

Wedge slowly ran his hand over his head, then nodded casually. "I do believe you are right," he replied.

He first joined National as a pilot during the war. Then, later, about the time Woody was running TACA in Central America, Wedge bought some war-surplus equipment and started his own airline in South America, a venture that collapsed during a revolution and forced his return to National.

Rosenthal first became associated with National in 1946, when he was a staff member of the Airlines Negotiating Conference, which, as the name implies, negotiated labor contracts for the member airlines. In 1948, he joined National as a full-time employee with the title of director of industrial relations, and after the conclusion of the ALPA strike, was elected a vice president. He is a handsome man with a speaking voice that would be the envy of any politician. A native of New York, he moved to Chicago in the early thirties, where he passed the bar examinations and went into law practice. Although his office was fairly close to the Bower-Baker Finance Company, he did not meet Baker until he became a specialist in airline labor relations.

Harry Taylor, who also is a native of New York, also became involved in the airline industry at the close of World War II, when he joined Pan American in its accounting division. He left Pan American in 1949 to become associated with the experimental carrier Resort Airlines, based in Miami. Resort was unique in that, although it was a certificated carrier, it could carry passengers only on an all-expense, "cruise" basis, in the same manner that cruise ships operate. In some circles, it is referred to as "Truman's airline," because authorization for the experiment was authorized by former President Harry Truman, and it collapsed shortly after Truman went out of office. Before Resort passed on, Taylor moved over to National as assistant to the treasurer, and he was elected vice president of properties in 1967. He is responsible for negotiating all leases in all of National's system cities, ranging from rentals of ticket offices to landing fees for the aircraft.

If anyone were to ask who runs the airline today, there undoubtedly would be a variety of answers. There is an executive committee made up of Maytag, Swim, and Truex. There are some who would point to this committee. There are others who would point to G. Ray Woody, because all the vice presidents report to him. Others, of course, would point to Bud Maytag, and although he put everything together, he probably would be the quickest to disagree.

The airline is run by everyone who is in it. Everyone has his own responsibility, and by doing it well, he is part of the group of some seven thousand employees who run the airline.

This is how Maytag runs the airline.

Today, there are eleven trunk carriers operating within the United States. When the Civil Aeronautics Board was created in 1938, there were nineteen trunk lines in existence, but within the past thirty years eight of them have collapsed or lost their identity through merger. Within the next decade, Maytag believes that another six or seven of the grandfather airlines will disappear. The cost of new equipment will be beyond the reach of the smaller trunks financially. Many of the carriers have already entered into pooling and leasing agreements in an attempt to meet mounting costs. National has entered into such an agreement with Pan American to exchange behemoth Boeing 747s according to seasonal demands for utilization, and with TWA on exchange of Boeing 727s.

National faces the same problems that face the industry in general. Traffic is increasing at the rate of approximately 15% annually. Its investment in capital equipment has increased incredibly, yet its profit levels are going down. Some years ago, the CAB determined that a fair rate of return upon investment was 10.5%. Today, the rate of return is closer to 7%. The CAB recently authorized a 4% increase in fares, but the increased competition along most of the nation's trunk routes may wipe out this advantage. Although this is an inflationary period, the cost of air transportation is almost 15% lower than it was six years ago.

Because of the problem of air traffic control at some of the nation's more urban airports, the Federal Aviation Agency has now stepped into another area of regulatory control by restricting schedules at certain airports such as New York,

Chicago, and Washington. With restricted scheduling, profits again will dip, and at a time when large reserves are needed to finance the purchase of new equipment.

Nevertheless, National still is a very healthy carrier. Under the first year of Maytag management, operating revenues were more than $82 million and profits more than $5 million. In 1968, operating revenues were approximately $224 million, with net profits of $21 million. Thus it seems that National is not going to be one of the six carriers that Maytag predicts will disappear within the next decade.

There are no more dramatics in the airline. The dramatics disappeared with the passing of its adolescence. One Boeing 747 can carry as many passengers on one flight as National carried during its entire first year of operations.

The airline has become mature. Now it must concern itself with the problem of not growing old prematurely, and the only way it can prevent this is by continued growth. The only way it can grow is through route expansion, and route expansion can be accomplished only through merger, purchase, or award from the Civil Aeronautics Board. Merger and purchase must also be accorded CAB approval.

The heart of the airline beats in the nation's capital, and the heart is an integral part of the anatomy.

INDEX